CHOICES

The Life of a Turkish Journalist

and

Finding Freedom in Exile

Sevgi Akarçeşme

Copyright © 2024 by Sevgi Akarçeşme

All rights reserved.

No portion of this publication may be reproduced, distributed, or transmitted in any form or by any means, including photocopying, recording, or other electronic or mechanical methods without prior written permission, except as permitted by U.S. copyright law. For permission requests, contact the author by email at sevgIstanbul@gmail.com.

For privacy reasons, some names have been withheld.

ISBN: 979-8-218-40879-4 (hardback)
ISBN: 979-8-218-40033-0 (paperback)

Dedicated to my mother, Mühibe

"What's past is prologue"
- William Shakespeare, *The Tempest*

There is evidence of human habitation in the region that includes the nation of Türkiye (formerly known to English speakers as Turkey) dating to the Paleolithic era. The geography between Southeastern Europe and Western Asia has long been valued for its strategic location offering access to waterways and trade routes. Several societies influenced its development, including Hellenistic, Roman, Persian, and Turkic civilizations.

Islam was already established in Anatolia (Asia Minor) before the rise of the Ottoman Empire, which controlled large areas of the Middle East, Eastern Europe, and North Africa for more than 600 years (1299-1922). Islam was dominant and was, to a large extent, the basis of a group identity in this diverse empire. It offered a foundation of values and norms for a multiethnic community. In contrast to Europe and other areas, however, religious uniformity was not imposed, as both a practical matter and a decision based on Islamic principle. Other religions were recognized and accommodated, though they occupied a secondary status.

The slow decline of Ottoman power in the late 18th century led to an interest in reform and Westernization, initially limited to the military and some aspects of commerce. The impetus grew when the once glorious superpower had become the "sick man of Europe" by the mid-19th century, and the resulting changes shook established notions of identity. Modernizations began to affect the entire society and weakened the power of religious scholars and leaders. There was disagreement over how best to address the problems facing the empire. The notion that modernity and success were intrinsically linked to a secular Western approach was contested, but gradually, the reformists began to gain more and more support. Their demands for democratization and an end to the monarchy became extreme, leading to revolution and violence at a delicate time. It would leave a lasting mark.

The Tanzimat reforms provided the seeds of the still-important emphasis on secularization and modernity, the role of the military in civil affairs, Turkish nationalism, the state bureaucracy, and religious identity. This is often overlooked, since the drive toward Westernization is most commonly associated with the founder of the Republic of Türkiye, Mustafa Kemal, who would become known by the adopted surname of Atatürk, or "father of Turks."

Atatürk was a brilliant military leader who was instrumental in the War of Independence and the creation of an entirely new state from the ruins of the empire and European colonialist interest in the territory. He was a reformist who swiftly instituted sweeping changes in the 1920s and 1930s that systematically dismantled Islam as the institutional basis of Turkish life and put the nation on a sharply defined course of transformation modeled after

Western Europe. While in some ways this formula can justly be described as beneficial, it was also authoritarian and not without pain.

Atatürk endeavored to create a nation state in which national consciousness rather than religion or ethnicity served as the primary determinant of identity. Society was forced to shift from perceiving itself as an essentially Muslim part of a vast empire into a modern, democratic, and secular nation-state. Islam was perceived as backward and the primary reason the empire had failed. Therefore, radical political, economic, and cultural reforms were implemented to fuse the population under a new singular identity and propel the country forward, compelling a fundamental shift in virtually all spheres of life.

The measures were profound, affecting everything from citizens' very names, the alphabet they used, and the way they dressed, to economic policy and the form of government and society from top to bottom. Muslim practices and symbols were abolished or relegated to the private sphere. Subjective identity and anchors to social belonging were ruthlessly invalidated and replaced in a matter of years. There were some legitimate reasons and intentions for this course of action, but the effects would be deep.

It is important to note that secularism in Türkiye is different from that of the U.S. and other countries. It includes not merely the separation of religion and state, but the subjugation of religion. It is not passive. It is the state's role to regulate and control the religious domain.

Similarly, the interpretation and practice of Islam are not universal. While the foundation is the same, they

SEVGİ AKARÇEŞME

manifest quite differently in various regions according to the historical and sociopolitical environment. Islam in Türkiye is distinct from that of Arab nations or Malaysia, for example.

This excessively brief history is insufficient to describe complex events and their effects, but it is important to have some recognition and comprehension of this background in order to understand today's Türkiye. Readers are encouraged to further explore the fascinating history of Türkiye, a country that continues to have an important position in world events. There is a rich literature of both fiction and nonfiction work.

CHAPTER 1

I blinked rapidly and the red lettering on the sign above the doorway no longer said "EXILE" but once again said "EXIT." Another blink and it said "EXIST," then "EXHALE." I was exhausted. Nervous, yet curiously detached, I could not examine existential emotions. They were contained, for the moment, as I waited to board a flight to an unknown future.

I had just made the painful decision to leave my home for a life in exile. I had wanted to be part of ushering my country into a new era of progress, but instead, I was compelled to flee. Numerous leaders, artists, and others have, of course, been forced into exile since ancient times, and Türkiye has been both host to those seeking refuge and the initiator of separation. I had not imagined I would become one of them, but here I was, persecuted by the government I had once defended. I could not help but wonder at the forces that brought me to this point. Beyond transient politics and personalities, I was drawn to consider other influences at play. History is not dry and remote. It not only repeats, it reverberates.

It has been said that the choices we make define us as individuals, but what defines the choices we are given? It is certainly true that the more mundane yet personally significant decisions about career and marriage, for example, have a great impact, let alone ethical and moral dilemmas we may face. From the time of our youth, the choices we make affect our future and we are accountable for the results.

In order to understand my own experience, I eventually began to evaluate the environmental elements of individual decisions and development, which have an enormous effect on this trajectory. We all contend with limitations and expectations that we do not necessarily comprehend or even have awareness of, yet which contribute to our personal identity and actions. Nuances of family and national history, such as memories and power structures, as well as cultural expectations and norms, including group trust and many other factors of the circumstances we experience, tend to have a strong influence on the choices we make.

In a sense, my story, and that of my family, reflect the development of modern Türkiye. In many ways, mine was a typical household: right-leaning and moderate Muslim in lifestyle, but open to urbanization and development. Like many Istanbul families, the roots of the Akarçeşme family originate elsewhere.

Available records, both personal and public, are limited, but we can definitively trace our ancestry to my paternal great-grandmother İpek, who was born in 1838 in the village of Kutluca, in the Giresun region located on the southern shore of the Black Sea. Census data indicate that İpek later moved to the nearby village of Dulundas, where my grandparents were born. A family tree document suggests that my paternal great-grandfather had been a blacksmith in the neighboring district of Gümüşhane before moving to Giresun.

CHOICES

At that time, European-style surnames were not required, though indications of status, profession, or lineage were used to identify individuals. One of the measures implemented following the creation of the independent state of Türkiye designed to homogenize and Westernize the population was the Surname Law of 1934. All citizens were required to adopt a fixed, hereditary surname.

Sıra	C	Yakınlık Derecesi	Adı	Soyadı	Baba Adı	Ana Adı	Doğum Yeri ve Tarihi	İl-İlçe-Mahalle/Köy	Cilt-Hane-Birey Sıra No	Medeni Hali	Durumu
1	K	Babasının Babasının Babasının Babasının Annesi	İPEK	-	OSMAN	ELİF	KUTLUCA 01/07/1838	Giresun/ Çamoluk/ DULUNDAS MAHALLESİ	26-17-5	Bekâr	Ölüm -
2	E	Babasının Annesinin Annesinin Babasının Babası	HÜSEYİN	-	MEHMET	EMİNE	YENİKÖY 01/07/1840	Giresun/ Çamoluk/ YENİKÖY KÖYÜ	72-47-1	Evli	Ölüm 18/10/1912
3	E	Annesinin Babasının Annesinin Babası	MEHMET	-	ALİ	RAHİME	HACIAHMETOĞLU 01/07/1844	Giresun/ Çamoluk/ HACIAHMETOĞLU KÖYÜ	35-10-1	Evli	Ölüm -
4	K	Babasının Annesinin Annesinin Babasının Annesi	AYŞE	-	MAHMUT	FATMA	YENİKÖY 01/07/1844	Giresun/ Çamoluk/ YENİKÖY KÖYÜ	72-47-7	Dul	Ölüm -
5	K	Babasının Annesinin Babasının Annesi	HÜSNİYE	-	HÜSEYİN	MAHİ	KARADİKMEN 01/07/1852	Giresun/ Çamoluk/ DULUNDAS MAHALLESİ	26-18-11	Dul	Ölüm 11/04/1937
6	K	Annesinin Babasının Annesinin Annesi	EMİNE	EKİNCİ	MUSTAFA	KAMER	KARADİKMEN 01/07/1854	Giresun/ Çamoluk/ HACIAHMETOĞLU KÖYÜ	35-10-3	Dul	Ölümün Tespiti -
7	E	Annesinin Babasının Babasının Babası	ALİ	-	HACI ABDURAHMAN	HANİFE HATUN	KALEDERE 01/07/1856	Giresun/ Çamoluk/ KALEDERE KÖYÜ	41-3-1	Evli	Ölüm 23/07/1916
8	K	Babasının Annesinin Babasının Annesi	HATİCE HATUN	KALELİ	MUSTAFA	KAMER HATUN	KARADİKMEN 01/07/1859	Giresun/ Çamoluk/ KALEDERE KÖYÜ	41-3-8	Dul	Ölüm 16/11/1949
9	E	Babasının Annesinin Annesinin Babası	HASAN	-	HÜSEYİN	AYŞE	YENİKÖY 01/07/1859	Giresun/ Çamoluk/ YENİKÖY KÖYÜ	72-47-2	Evli	Ölüm 08/01/1921

Government genealogical record

Notably, it was mandated that the surname be Turkish; surnames of another origin were no longer permitted. The law stipulated that as the head of the household, the eldest male would choose the surname. In the event of his absence or incapacitation, the wife was to choose the surname. Family lore indicates that my surname, which means "flowing fountain (or natural spring)," was selected by the man who was considered the wisest and most educated in the village because my ancestors lived near a water source, an important landmark in the village, using a naming convention similar to that of Native Americans and others.

Akarçeşme is not a common surname. I have always liked it, though proper pronunciation outside Türkiye has proved difficult. I did, however, come to regret that its uniqueness meant that members of my family could be very easily identified once I had become a target of President Recep Tayyip Erdoğan. For this reason, I do not name my siblings, who are currently in Türkiye, in this book. Retribution against family members of those in disfavor with his government is not uncommon. It is only a small measure of protection, but all I can provide.

My mother's family had lived in Giresun for generations, but an unsubstantiated story asserts that their lineage traces back to the family of a feudal lord named Karaosmanoğlu, which had been exiled to the more isolated province from the more prosperous western region of Türkiye. The Karaosmanoğlus were at one time one of the most powerful families in Anatolia; however, they lost most of their influence under the centralization and reform that took place during the reign of Mahmud

II (1808-1839). Descendants now live in many areas, including Giresun, but while possible, my own connection to this line is unconfirmed.

After the death of Atatürk, the country's founding father, in 1938, his longtime friend, Mustafa İsmet İnönü, succeeded him and became the nation's second president. İnönü had been a successful military commander and statesman, serving alongside Atatürk in the early years of the republic. The parliament granted him the official title of National Chief (Millî Şef).

He largely maintained the comprehensive reforms imposed by Atatürk and pushed the new country forward by many measures, but the transition to a secular and more modern state was not without challenges, both internal and external. Statist policies and further nationalization of the economy were substituted for the initial, more liberal economic policies in response to the Great Depression and other difficulties. Industrialization progressed, but the economy deteriorated under the weight of lost foreign trade and the effects of World War II.

Given its strategic location, both the Axis and the Allied powers courted Türkiye as an ally, but Türkiye was cautious and maintained neutrality until February 1945, when it joined the Allies. Complicated historical relations with the European principals and concerns about Türkiye's status and its future justified apprehension. President İnönü drove a hard bargain with the Allies.

This association was to prove beneficial, but it would also be significant long after the post-war period. Suspicion of the intentions of foreigners, the threat of destabilization and dismemberment, and a sensitivity to being used and seen as inferior continue today. Turks are proud, and admirably very mindful of history, though it is not always a strictly accurate or balanced view, and skepticism is prevalent. But this is true in much of the world. As always, it is worth asking, "Who determines what is accurate?"

The challenging circumstances of economic stagnation and recovery from prolonged war and impoverishment in the 1940s prompted my paternal grandfather, Ali, born in about 1932, to migrate from Giresun to Istanbul. Western Türkiye was then and remains a long-standing site of wealth generation and concentration that draws those from the countryside seeking opportunity. There was frequently little choice but to relocate, and this often meant Istanbul. Those who were children in the early years of the republic describe years of extreme poverty and other hardships. My grandfather Ali often recounted the story of his journey to Istanbul by ship alone at age 14. At that time, there were few roads linking the rural regions to cities.

Like many migrants, Ali had great ambitions and he was eager and enterprising in his efforts to succeed. I have always admired his optimism, drive, and zest for life. Upon arrival, he shared accommodation with other young men from the countryside who had also come to the unfamiliar city with big dreams.

Ali started as a worker in the coal and wood trade and was able to open a small business of his own in that sector within a few years. A marriage was arranged for Ali at age 16 with a young woman named Hayriye, who was from the same village (Dulundas). For the first several years of their marriage she remained in Giresun and Ali continued to travel back and forth from Istanbul to visit. Regional affiliations continue to be very important and still provide a powerful sense of identity and support to Turks today.

Also in the late 1940s, significant opposition to the policies of the ruling Republican People's Party (CHP) government led to the formation of a new political party, the first opposition party to endure and succeed. Adnan Menderes, the son of a wealthy landowner and a former member of the CHP, demanded more political and democratic freedom. Assurances of liberalization and progress had strong appeal, particularly among those who struggled economically. A Menderes slogan that would be remembered decades later was the promise of a millionaire in every neighborhood. In 1950, in the country's first free elections, the Democrat Party (DP) won 52 percent of the vote and Menderes became prime minister, the first non-CHP leader.

Marshall Plan funding and other foreign financing enabled Menderes to make large investments in agriculture, finance, energy, and education, among other areas. Housing as well as road and highway construction were also features of the early years of the Menderes government. He fulfilled important promises that improved people's daily lives. When I was growing up, my grandfather used to tell me about how Menderes built wonderful wide avenues and boulevards, such as those named Vatan (homeland) and Millet (nation/people of the nation), which remain major traffic arteries in Istanbul to this day.

The economy was strong in the early years of Menderes's tenure and development was welcomed. Istanbul continued to grow in population as well. Between

1950 and 1955, the population of the city saw an increase of 55 percent, reaching 1.5 or 1.6 million. It was only as an adult that I learned that the infrastructure projects were frequently completed at the expense of historic Ottoman sites. The attitude that progress trumps heritage, particularly when there are immediate economic concerns, continues today, though appreciation for the preservation of historical sites and the environment is growing, while still very limited in power.

Menderes was also a hero to many because he enabled greater religious freedom, which was welcomed by those who had chafed under the CHP's repression of religious expression. He reopened and built many mosques, reinstated the public call to prayer in Arabic rather than Turkish, and built relations with Muslim states. Even many who were less religiously observant but claimed a Muslim identity, such as my grandfather, approved of the relaxation of the strict anti-religious measures of the Kemalist (inspired by Atatürk) regimes.

The 1950s were pivotal years in my family's life and for the nation. Late in the decade, Hayriye joined her husband in Istanbul with their first two children, my father, Hasan, and their second son, Hüseyin, who were born in 1953 and 1955, respectively. As sweet as my grandfather has been to his grandchildren, he was apparently a rather typically authoritarian father. For boys born to a poor family in the mid-1950s, there was a firm expectation that Hasan and Hüseyin would work in their father's tiny coal-sales office after leaving school. I saw that Ali wanted to control his sons even in adulthood. My father and my uncle Hüseyin have said that there were occasional beatings when they were young, and while I never saw him strike my grandmother, in later life, she spoke of some domestic abuse.

Paternalism and sexism were essentially considered acceptable and almost normal in society. Even today, though there is a strong movement in support of women's rights, women who report abuse are often merely sent home, women are often discouraged from working after marriage, told not to be too assertive or independent, and inequalities are largely accepted. In 2014, Deputy Prime Minister Bülent Arinç said that women should not laugh loudly in public and should preserve their decency and chasteness at all times in a complaint about moral decline. The scolding provoked an uproar and a social media protest of women posting photos and videos of themselves laughing. Yet the rate of domestic violence and femicide in Türkiye has grown alarmingly in recent years.

My grandmother was illiterate, and my grandfather, by his account, attended primary school for only three months. It was the education he received during his two years of mandatory military service that gave him the ability to read and write well enough to succeed in business. This was not unusual. In a predominantly rural country where one started work very early in life, military service often served as a substitute school for men and was an efficient nation-building tool.

Then, as now, especially in rural Türkiye, young men who have not completed their military service are often not considered mature enough to marry. The mandatory period of service had been reduced to 18 months when my father served and has been further minimized since then. There is now also the option to pay for an exemption, and it has not gone unnoticed that the majority of those serving and dying for their country are from less privileged backgrounds.

Military service also results in a delayed entry into or a pause in professional life, and some question the need for the requirement. There is an argument to be made for the potential benefits of a period of service, both to the individual and to the state, but the indoctrination of nationalist sentiment and the desire to maintain a ready force for operations, though much of the public often finds them unnecessary, are doubtless still factors that will prohibit elimination of compulsory service in Türkiye for the foreseeable future.

Civil-military relations in Türkiye have been fraught since the foundation of the nation. A system of military tutelage with frequent interventions in the political sphere is a primary reason for incomplete democratization. Civilian politicians had to share power with military officers. The military has seen itself as a guardian of the state and acted with impunity until very recently.

Influential civilians embraced assertive secularist, Turkish nationalist, and anti-communist ideologies, which contributed to fears of "Islamic reactionary," "Kurdish separatist," and "communist" threats. They regarded military oversight of politics as the most effective way to eliminate these threats. A certain degree of insecurity and suspicion prompted by history and geography continues to be a relevant factor in the Turkish psyche, and the elite often do not trust the electoral choices of the majority.

CHOICES

Though his parents had little formal education and prioritized employment as the basis of success, my father excelled in school and even secured a scholarship for entry into an esteemed public high school established in 1872, Vefa High School. Since his mother was illiterate and his father was very busy, Hasan's elementary school teacher assisted him with the application. However, he eventually dropped out. When I asked him why he did not finish high school, he vaguely hinted at the challenges of class differences. He is reluctant to discuss his life in detail.

My uncle Hüseyin also went to a public high school for a while, but similarly discontinued his studies because of my grandfather's expectations that he would work. If I remember correctly, my uncle was very upset about this and was determined to get his high school degree. I remember that he took night classes to learn English, even though it was not required in the family profession. Both my father and my uncle Hüseyin successfully developed both the family business and independently augmented their education in the commercial world. They came from a traditional family, yet they welcomed new ideas and accepted differences.

Though the literacy rate in Türkiye is now well over 90 percent, proficiency among older adults is often still weak, particularly in rural areas. Atatürk's reforms included free, compulsory primary education and thousands of schools were opened across the country. The education of girls and women was encouraged. It was a state tool to promote development, modernization, and secularization, but it was not always observed, either by choice or by circumstance.

Over time, the introduction of neoliberal policies and conservative religious ideology significantly altered the system. However, both perspectives have emphasized forms of nationalism and a limited definition of collective identity that marginalized minorities. Beginning in 1933, students were required to recite a pledge each day that begins with "I am a Turk" and ends with the statement "How proud is the one who can say 'I am a Turk!'" This became controversial and was eventually repealed in 2013, reinstated in 2018, then removed once again in 2021.

The economic success and optimism of the early 1950s did not last; economic difficulties began to emerge, and Menderes began to tighten control. Criticism was not tolerated, and media and government opponents were censored. Rising inflation was fuel for additional nationalist sentiment and discontent. Greek and other populations that had lived in Istanbul for centuries were targeted in a deadly riot in 1955, which accelerated the Turkification and exodus of "others" initiated years earlier, as well as some disappointment in Menderes.

Despite a shared history—or in some ways because of it—the relationship between Türkiye and Greece has always been complicated. Though Istanbul still hosts the ecumenical patriarchate of the Eastern Orthodox Church, also known as the Patriarchate of Constantinople, the current Greek population has been reduced to a few thousand. Sporadic disagreements over territory and other concerns, sometimes with enormous effects, such as the population exchange of 1923, have arisen since the days of the Ottoman Empire and continue to this day.

The dramatic social changes and urban transformation of the Menderes years stoked fear among the military and other elites that the staunchly secular orientation of Kemalism would be supplanted. In addition to granting more freedom to Muslims, Menderes considered seeking Russian financial assistance given the economic woes, which inflamed anti-communist sentiment. In the face of growing unrest, Menderes established the Commission of Inquiries (also referred to as the Committee of Inquest), made up entirely of members of his own DP party and tasked with investigation of the opposition party (CHP) and the press, which further exacerbated animosity and demonstrated a clear shift toward authoritarianism from the earlier champion of democracy. The panel had the authority to act as prosecutor and deliver a verdict that could not be appealed, violating the separation of powers. Rumors circulated that the CHP plotted revolution, political activities were banned, and the press was censored. Protests and violence continued.

In 1961, Menderes and two of his cabinet members, Hasan Polatkan and Fatin Rüştü Zorlu, were tried, convicted, and executed by hanging following a coup in 1960 launched by a group within the military. One of the coup leaders was allegedly a member of a US-trained "stay-behind" group. He supported a return to military leadership of the country, but was outweighed by those, including other members of the military, who demanded democracy and a multiparty system. In what would be a recurring scenario, purges, trials, accusations of treason, misuse of public funds, and abrogation of the constitution surfaced and resulted in turmoil.

Türkiye was an original signatory to the U.N. Charter in 1945 and was admitted to NATO in 1952. While not entirely acknowledged by governments, there is evidence to suggest that in the period following World War II, clandestine "stay-behind" forces were created in most member states, including Türkiye, as a part of NATO's anti-communist efforts. These groups were meant to be the foundation for a resistance movement in the event of communist invasion and occupation.

Based in the military, but eventually including civilians, these secretive cells were provided with arms and trained in sabotage and guerrilla warfare, conducting terrorist attacks, and the use of propaganda. These efforts are alleged to have included designs to blame and discredit the left in order to justify increased state authoritarianism and nationalism. This is part of the origin of what is referred to in Türkiye as the "deep state."

The roots of such an organization and both fear and admiration of its strength are deep in Türkiye, dating at least to the Ottoman Janissaries, an elite infantry unit of the sultan that wielded great power, both military and political, as well as groups that were preparing for resistance following World War I and became part of the independence movement.

Precise details remain unknown, but some version of a deep state in Türkiye was apparently supported by Western allies and for decades its existence was truly unknown to most, even at the highest levels. Once it became part of the popular consciousness, however, it would become a common and useful catch-all bogeyman. Various events have been blamed on the deep state, and there may be elements of truth to at least some of the accusations, but we may never know the full truth.

Menderes had been a hero in the eyes of much of the general public; that is, the traditional majority of right-wing conservatives, and after his death, many sons were named after him, but for years the 1960 coup was excused and celebrated. It was not until the 1990s that he was officially pardoned and the state apologized to the Menderes family. I remember the jubilation when a mausoleum was erected in Istanbul to commemorate Menderes and the two ministers who were executed alongside him. It has great symbolic value as a means of protesting Kemalist militarism.

Modern Turkish history is full of episodes in which its own citizens were victimized, only to be cherished much later when it was too late. In perfect accordance with the tendency to describe everything in black or white, there is often no room for shades of gray when it comes to figures like Menderes. He is either a hero or an authoritarian leader, depending on where one's opinions fall on the political spectrum.

Too often, immediate concerns supersede what are perceived as grand and idealistic ideas, including concepts like freedom of expression and the rule of law. More than half a century later, we can see a similar pattern of inflexible views with little regard for nuance or imperfection in Türkiye. Current President Erdoğan is typically either adored or despised. Those who "insult" the president are still prosecuted, and it is still something of a taboo to criticize the idolized Atatürk, even among those who complain about Erdoğan's one-man rule and speak of Atatürk as a man who ruled the country with an iron fist. Years-long indoctrination and strongman rule can inhibit objectivity.

There are interesting parallels between Menderes and Erdoğan. Common elements include populism, a largely rural and religious base, emphasis on construction and development, improvements to daily life, economic crisis, fears of a military coup, and friction over secularism. Erdoğan has borrowed directly from Menderes when he invokes the "will of the people" to justify harsh treatment of opponents and the denial of rights.

Yet in recent years, Erdoğan has also come to, at least when convenient, embrace aspects of Kemalism. The security sector once again rose to prominence in public life once the power of the military had been clipped. For example, Erdoğan reverted to the state's original rationale that a military solution is the only appropriate response to demands for rights and autonomy for the Kurdish minority.

One month after the execution of Menderes in 1961, which was deplored abroad, a general election was held and administrative authority was returned to civilians under İnönü, the leader of the opposition CHP, but the military continued to dominate the political scene. There was considerable discontent all around, leading to the growth of leftist organizations, increased resentment among pious Muslims, and two failed military coup attempts in 1962 and 1963 launched by radical elements within the military who were dissatisfied with the coalition of the CHP, the DP, and others.

The Justice Party (AP) was founded in 1961 as a replacement for the DP, which had been banned, and my grandfather and many others ardently supported its populist leader, Süleyman Demirel, who was elected prime minister in 1965 in the first free election since 1960.

CHOICES

Unlike Menderes, however, Demirel came from a poor, rural background. He was the first prime minister to have been born in the new Turkish republic, and in a sense, as a civil engineer and a success, he was a symbol of the greater opportunity available since the sultanate had been abolished. He would go on to have a long and influential impact on Turkish politics. Perhaps my earliest political memory is reading about Demirel in the newspaper. I can recall looking at black-and-white photos of him in the mid-1980s wondering if his hand was really made of metal because the surname Demirel means "iron hand."

During the 1960s, the Akarçeşme family continued a relatively rapid transition to urban life. Ali and his wife, Hayriye, had a third son, Mehmet, and their only daughter, Yıldız, born in Istanbul in 1961 and 1967, respectively. Mehmet had a twin brother, Ahmet, who died as an infant. The boys' names are typical of a Turkish Muslim family, but Yıldız, which means "star," was a rather modern name.

Traditional names commonly have a religious or historical reference, but over time, nouns came to be used as first names much more commonly than in the U.S. They often express aspirations or symbolize the relationship to the land. For example, common names include Barış (peace), Bilge (wise), Can (soul/life), Cesur (brave/gallant), Özgür (free), Umut (hope), Dilek (wish/desire), Doğan (falcon), Deniz (sea), Güneş (sun), and combinations, such as Ayşegül, which joins Ayşe, the Turkish form of the Arabic name Aisha, a wife of Prophet Muhammad, with a word of Persian origin meaning "flower" or "rose."

Themes are also commonplace, such as giving siblings the names Cloud and Rain, or even War and Peace. In addition to the ordinary significance and considerations parents may give to naming their child, Turkish names can also be highly politicized. At times, names rooted in Arabic, Kurdish, or other languages have been forbidden, and even today, names can carry a burden of association that is not always welcome over time. One family famously named their triplets Recep, Tayyip, and Erdoğan.

The Akarçeşme family, 1963
(My father is standing behind his parents)

At some point, likely in the 1960s, my grandfather Ali also worked as a bus driver for the Istanbul Municipality as a second job. There, he got into the habit of wearing more formal business clothing every day. I have never seen my grandfather wear anything but a jacket and tie during the day, even though he was dealing with blue collar workers.

He is such an interesting character. He is a proud man who achieved a lot through hard work during very difficult times. "I had two jobs while all my peers had only one," he often said to us. All of his grandchildren grew up listening to his stories about how he came to the city as a poor teenager and built a family business selling coal and wood.

My grandfather Ali is self-centered, controlling, and tends to take credit for everything that went well in his life, but unlike many of his contemporaries, he did listen to what my grandmother had to say. She was the real boss of the family in some ways. Despite his façade of strength and stoicism, my grandfather recognized that his success, defined by him as making money, was due to their teamwork.

However, as they grew older, he began to disparage his ailing wife for not being able to "keep up with his pace" and not being "urban" enough. Still, he did not want to leave home without her. After all, they were a couple who tied the knot when they were only 16 years old and went through thick and thin together for all of their adult lives. My grandfather was devastated when Hayriye died

With my paternal grandparents, 2014

in the fall of 2016, leaving him alone. Ali is now in his 90s, and regrettably, I can now only see him in rare video calls.

Demirel's government pushed Türkiye into the industrial era and achieved an annual economic growth rate of 6 percent a year. He was re-elected in 1969, but recession and the formation of splinter groups within his party diminished his parliamentary majority and brought the legislative process to a halt. By 1970, social unrest caused by conflicts between pro-Islamic parties on the right, and Kurds, students, and workers demanding radical reform on the left, had become quite violent.

The population was scared by the extreme chaos and the military was agitated. The military again exercised its role of protector, and in 1971, Demirel was forced out of office in a coup "by memorandum." It was essentially an ultimatum and indicated that the armed forces would take control if the government could not restore satisfactory order. Demirel resigned, but what would follow remained uncertain. Successive governments failed to manage the rising instability, and the pragmatist Demirel was back in power in 1975, with the backing of both nationalists and Islamists.

By the late 1970s, having completed their military service, tradition held that it was time for my father and my uncle Hüseyin to marry. My grandmother chose their brides. My mother, Mühibe, was known to my grandmother through social circles, and for Hüseyin, she selected her own niece. Arranged marriage and marriage to a cousin were not uncommon, but my mom always felt that her mother-in-law favored my uncle's wife because of the family relationship. I can recall a certain tension in the family from even my early childhood memories.

CHOICES

The brothers were married in a joint ceremony on October 8, 1977, at a wedding hall called "Casablanca," which was apparently a popular venue at the time in the heart of the central and historic Taksim area of Istanbul's Beyoğlu district. My grandparents spoke proudly of this shared wedding as something special. If you ask my mother, however, it was just an attempt by her in-laws to save money and she resented not having her own special ceremony.

My father was 25 and my mother was only 17 when they were married. This was not unusual at the time, and while the average age of marriage in Türkiye has risen in recent years in parallel with the rise in education and urbanization, teenaged or even younger brides are still seen in more traditional or rural families. For many young girls in Türkiye, particularly those who lack access to higher education and financial independence, marriage and motherhood is the expected and sometimes only viable or valued path in life.

CHAPTER 2

On January 11, 1979, Hasan and Mühibe had the first of their five children, Ali and Hayriye's first grandchild. I was a premature baby, and it was not certain that I would live. I weighed only 1.5 kilograms (3.3 pounds) and measured 35 centimeters (14 inches) in length at birth. My family was very fortunate to have access to a hospital with incubators and good medical care. My survival and the joy of both my family and the caring staff at the hospital where I stayed for a month after birth inspired my name, Sevgi, which means "love," "compassion," or "affection."

At that time, Türkiye had a largely closed, protected economy. As a result, access to imported goods was a privilege. My mother has always regretted not being able to breastfeed me due to my premature birth, but I remember that my family was proud to be able to give me SMA infant formula, which was probably not available to everyone.

I was small, fragile, and prone to illness throughout my childhood. Fortunately, my family was able to afford a private pediatrician, Dr. Gülsen Erhan. She was my doctor for many years, and always joked that the early fears of potential problems with brain function had been mistaken. The story of my early arrival and survival was told to relatives and friends repeatedly over the years, and many who know me have wondered if that might explain my impatience and persistence.

There has never been a prolonged period that was truly stable and peaceful in modern Turkish history, but existing tensions in society became exceedingly turbulent in the late 1970s. Social unrest between leftist groups demanding radical reform, such as students, workers, and importantly, Kurdish separatists, as well as some on the right, particularly ultranationalists, reached an unprecedented level of violence.

Social instability was fueled by a failing economy unable to adequately manage urban migration, oil prices, foreign debt, and more, and political dysfunction ensued. Coalition governments led by Demirel and Bülent Ecevit, a left-of-center secularist who was also a poet, repeatedly failed. Though a CHP parliamentarian, Ecevit was a Eurosceptic and various initiatives irritated both the left and the right.

Longstanding hostilities and discord in Cyprus between the Greek and Turkish populations and the legacy of British rule had also come to a head. Ecevit's decision to intervene militarily in 1974 contributed to a victory for Ecevit and the CHP over Demirel in the 1977 general election.

Political violence and disruption continued, however, including numerous assassination attempts, and the massacre of leftist protesters in Taksim Square and members of the Alevi branch of Islam (a minority in Türkiye) in Kahramanmaraş, and Ecevit ultimately resigned in 1979 in the face of instability and allegations of corruption. He speculated about the role of the deep state in events, but he, too, would go on to have a lasting influence in politics. Demirel returned to the premiership without a majority.

Volatility, fear of radical influences, and violence were widespread. My grandfather's tiny office in a coal warehouse was bombed by far-left activists because he had expressed support for Demirel. At the time, my mother was pregnant with my first sister. In September 1980, less than a year after Ecevit's resignation, the military once again deposed the government and assumed the role of guardian of the state.

With my mother, 1979

In the face of daily killings in the streets and the perceived threat of communism, which was considered even worse than a religious influence, the military coup that ousted Demirel was largely welcomed by the general public. Across the spectrum, the public was fed up with "anarchists," strikes, food lines and crippling inflation, a dysfunctional and partially paralyzed parliament, and social tension. Efforts to implement and sustain a mixed economy had been insufficient to surmount the many challenges of the time, including the increase in world oil prices and a debt crisis.

The restoration of order, led by stiff-necked Chief of the General Staff General Kenan Evren, was largely accepted and appreciated, but the military takeover would later be viewed as a stain. Evren is the first president I remember. He was a fierce Kemalist, but also used Islamist rhetoric. Severe restrictions and revisions were implemented to re-establish order, but in the immediate aftermath of the coup, the extent of the repression and its objectives were not contested or even widely known.

**With my first sister and cousins, early 1980s
(I am standing at far left)**

Both Ecevit and Demirel were prosecuted under martial law, and arrests, torture, executions, and purges were common. Parliament was suspended and all political parties were disbanded with their leaders taken into custody. Local governors and other civil servants were replaced by military personnel. Workers' strikes were made illegal and labor unions were barred. A curfew was imposed in the evening and leaving the country was prohibited.

Civil liberties and dissent were crushed, and a new constitution was imposed that gave the military virtually unlimited power and condoned institutional prejudice against minorities. Kurds in particular, and anyone deemed an "enemy of the state," were frequently subjected to mistreatment in pre-trial detention.

Human rights abuses were institutionalized under the emphasis on reinstating "traditional" values, a secular Turkish nationalism that recognized a role of Islam, as a counterweight to Marxism. Stability was regained and there was a welcome economic turnaround, but at a huge cost that would have unanticipated consequences. The effects of the intervention had a direct impact on the rise of both the Kurdistan Workers' Party (PKK) and political Islamism.

In 1984, the PKK began a more concerted insurgency against the Turkish government. Formed in the 1970s as a socialist Kurdish separatist movement, in part in response to suppression of Kurdish culture, the conflict has been an enduring source of pain and loss of life ever since, claiming at least 40,000 lives.

Kurds have lived for millennia in an area that now comprises portions of Iran, Iraq, Syria, and Türkiye. The Treaty of Sèvres, which redrew borders after World War I and the collapse of the Ottoman Empire, included an independent Kurdish state; however, the superseding

Treaty of Lausanne, negotiated by İnönü, eliminated this provision and the Kurds became a minority in all of the newly defined nations, with history and family ties that crossed borders.

A separate Kurdish identity was consistently denied. Kurds in Türkiye were called "mountain Turks" and various efforts to relocate residents and repopulate the area ensued, as well as revolts. In the post-1980-coup era, the Kurdish language was officially prohibited, and use in any form often led to imprisonment and discrimination.

The struggle for some measure of equal rights and recognition became very bloody. In the 1990s the PKK officially reduced its ambitions for independence to a semi-autonomous region within the Turkish state; however, violence, mistrust, and discrimination continue.

I don't remember absorbing or understanding much of the turmoil of the immediate period after the 1980 coup, but I was a curious child and liked to read everything. I remember being fascinated by newspapers even before I learned to read and write. At that time, even in Istanbul, kindergarten was not accessible to many. Most of those from my generation or previous generations who attended kindergarten were likely from an educated and wealthy family.

I do not remember having financial difficulties, but in terms of formal education and position, my family was certainly not among the most privileged. Nevertheless, at home and in the office, we bought newspapers every day. When I became frustrated because I did not understand what was in the "photo novels," I would ask my mother and other family members to read them aloud to me.

Though my family was conservative, they read the unwaveringly secular *Hürriyet* daily, whose editors and columnists were against any public display of piety and regularly featured photos of women in revealing clothing and bikinis. That was, and is, the general attitude of many Turkish families, no matter how traditional their religious beliefs. It is interesting to me that supposedly serious publications find it necessary to include sensational photos and stories, but that formula of relying on sex, scandal, and blood to drive sales is an unfortunate reality in journalism, even under an Islamist government.

In addition to *Hürriyet*, my family also subscribed to the conservative daily newspaper *Türkiye*. I remember eagerly awaiting the children's magazine and reading the two-page stories that explained and demonstrated religious virtue. The *Türkiye* daily also distributed free religious books and tapes to its subscribers. I can recall reading about the life of Prophet Muhammad for the first time in one of these books. I remember being intrigued by the illustrations of life in the desert, a completely unfamiliar world for a child from Istanbul.

I was very impressed by the description of Prophet Muhammad's childhood and how God provided shade and protection in the form of a cloud that followed him to provide relief from the sun wherever he went. I also remember the strong impact of the accounts of the prophet's character. Throughout his life he was known for his reliability, even by his enemies. All of this was communicated without images of him, since most Muslims avoid visual depictions of any of the prophets, including Moses and Abraham.

Despite the emphasis on symbols in the majority of the Muslim world, from an early age I tended to pay more attention to the moral dimension of Islam. Muslims are taught that the rights of others are inalienable and that even God will not forgive the violation of those rights, but in many of today's Muslim societies, this rule seems to have been largely neglected or forgotten. In fact, many Muslims who have experienced Western societies agree that non-Muslim Westerners are more inclined to protect the rights of individuals, whether or not they are obligated to do so.

I can see that I was influenced to live a devout life to avoid God's wrath from a young age, but I value and continue to hold this belief. There were also secular influences in my youth, and in some ways, it would have been easier for me had I put my faith aside, but I am grateful for the foundation it gave me and the guidance it provides.

CHAPTER 3

Though I remember President Evren, my memories of the politics of the early 1980s are more closely tied to a prime minister, Turgut Özal, who won the first post-coup election in 1983. Özal had been an influential actor promoting economic reform as an undersecretary for Demirel and had served as a state minister and deputy prime minister in the interim military government. He established the Motherland Party (ANAP) after the existing political parties were banned by the provisional government.

The generals had hinted at another party for the voters, but ANAP emerged successful in the first election after the restoration of democratic rights. Özal was short, fat, congenial, and importantly, a civilian politician with both a deeply religious yet dedicated secular view. He saw no contradiction in those beliefs. Özal had valuable experience in state planning and at the World Bank, and he was able to provide real benefits. He was generally popular. I may have been influenced by propaganda, but he not only opened the economy, he also tried to engage in a resolution of the extremely sensitive topics of the Armenian genocide and negotiations with the PKK. He ultimately had a tremendous impact, though it was not easy.

CHOICES

My family liked Özal, in part because of the unprecedented economic liberalization he initiated in the mid-1980s. My father and uncles worked hard, and like many other entrepreneurs, they were able to expand the tiny coal-sales office that my grandfather had started. They prospered when Özal lifted protectionist measures, which made it much easier to export as well as import foreign goods, among other changes.

I can remember how rare foreign brands had been and how tempting the European chocolates were that our distant relatives in Germany brought us during their summer vacations in Türkiye when they were not available to us. Not everyone could afford it, but under Özal's government, the population was introduced to consumer diversification and many families flourished. My grandfather, however, as an ardent supporter of Demirel, the populist leader of the center-right and Özal's political rival, never warmed to Özal.

In the 1980s, the state held a monopoly over television, and a lot of regime propaganda was broadcast on TV. For many years, the state-owned TV broadcast began and ended with a performance of the national anthem at the tomb of Atatürk. I bet I was not the only kid who stood up when the national anthem was played, even on TV. The pervasive indoctrination was so strong that I cried more than once on the anniversary of Atatürk's death, even though he died in 1938. Sometimes children who laughed or did not pay attention during respectful commemorative ceremonies at school were disciplined. The dates of Atatürk's birth and death and the names of his parents were one of the first things children learned in school.

SEVGİ AKARÇEŞME

While it is certainly admirable to learn about the founder of the nation, few Turks could or would have questioned a level of reverence usually only found in countries like North Korea. The anniversary of Atatürk's death is still recognized publicly, not merely with a formal ceremony, but by members of the public who stop what they are doing for a moment of veneration. On the morning of November 10, every year it is still common to see traffic halt briefly while drivers exit their vehicles and stand in respect, people pause on the sidewalk or in their work, and sirens and horns sound to recognize the precise moment that Atatürk died.

Though the degree of devotion has lessened somewhat in recent years, it is still very powerful. Atatürk provokes strong feelings and can be a difficult subject to discuss with any objectivity. In my first year of study at one of the country's most liberal universities, a British teacher forbade us to write about Atatürk on the grounds that no one could be detached in their evaluation.

The evening news in those days started with statements from the president and the prime minister. All governments of whatever stripe benefited from an information monopoly; the majority of airtime was allocated to the ruling party. Prime Minister Özal addressed the public in a special broadcast titled *From the Executive* (İcraatın İçinden) to explain how he was moving the country forward. Citizens were often reminded that Türkiye desperately needed national unity and solidarity. While true, this cliché continues to be used by those in power to sustain and retain their position, as is control of media outlets.

I remember watching the limited programming available on one and then two television channels, initially in black and white. I also recall listening to children's game shows broadcast by state radio stations on a huge, old-fashioned radio. It was during the Özal years that television, like so much else, changed dramatically. The arrival of color TV was a big deal for millions of kids like me.

Circa 1986

However, the exciting progress hid some very dark activities. Torture conducted in the prison of the Kurdish city of Diyarbakır was so inhumane that there is now a broad consensus that it contributed to the growth of PKK violence. The 1980 coup had led to brutal suppression of critical political activity. The previous infighting between the left and right wings had been eliminated because anyone who engaged in any form of unacceptable political activity was persecuted.

Certain singers were banned in an effort to protect social order. Transgender singer Bülent Ersoy and Kurdish singer İbrahim Tatlıses were not permitted to perform on TV, even when Tatlıses sang in Turkish. Interestingly, today, both are Erdoğan supporters. Many artists previously alleged to hold communist views had already been forced into exile and some had their citizenship revoked, but even non-political singers were banned from public stations if they were not considered representatives of the desired "higher" culture.

Probably at least in part as a result of rapid migration from rural parts of Turkey, especially to Istanbul, arabesque folk music became increasingly visible in society. This style of music uses traditional instruments and is typically very emotional, often containing themes of love and working-class struggles. Arabesque also included forbidden non-Western influences. It would become broadly popular and yet also viewed as almost treasonous by some, but it reflected some of the frustrations and disappointments of the new city-dwellers. In some ways it plays the part seen in variations of traditional folk music originating in many countries, such as fado in Portugal and the blues genre in the U.S.

Arabesque musicians found an audience through audio and video cassettes. People often gathered in the home of one of the few with a video cassette player. Child stars like "Little Emrah," "Little Ceylan," and the popular actor and comedian Kemal Sunal became very successful despite the bans on national broadcast. Sunal was a favorite of children at the time, and I was no exception. I do not know if the increasingly political tone in his films was a reason for some to be banned, but he typically portrayed a loveable, somewhat bumbling, naive working-class hero with humor and a truth that no doubt provided comic relief and reflected hardships familiar to many migrants.

Özal became the first civilian to be elected to the presidency in 1989 and took advantage of the years of suppressed political activity. He emphasized unity among all political currents, but he was unable to integrate Kurdish demands for a separate identity into democratic channels. Armed conflict with the PKK grew and became a source of great bitterness and long-lasting enmity on both sides. Inflation also became a significant problem and there was eventually widespread criticism that he had forsaken the new middle class and there were accusations of corruption.

By the time I was 11, I had three younger sisters. Since my first sister was only a year younger than I, we were raised almost like twins, though there were stark differences in character. She was much more vivacious, and we often quarreled as youngsters. My second sister has always been quiet and responsible. The youngest of the girls was the most spoiled of us all. I took an active interest in their education and tried to motivate them to dream big and achieve, and they all graduated from university, but they are not eager to leave their comfort zones.

My brother, the youngest child, was born in 1999 with mild physical and cognitive impairments. I believe that his potential development was somewhat restricted by conditions at home and the scarcity of special education opportunities, even in private schools. My father always expected him to be like any other boy, and my mother always overprotected him. I think both approaches were unfortunate, but it was hard to change my parents' inclinations.

If he had been born and raised in a more advanced Western country, he would have learned the skills to more fully integrate with society, but while this is slowly changing in Türkiye, these opportunities are still much more limited. Sadly, general attitudes toward disabilities continue to be somewhat antiquated and disempowering. My brother largely remains within the protective walls of home.

It was during the early 1990s that we heard about the concept of private TV channels. I must have been in fifth grade or so when there was talk about a new TV channel in addition to the state-owned TRT. I still remember the confusion and curiosity. How could another channel even exist? One of Özal's sons was a partner in the first private TV channel, even though private broadcast violated the constitution at the time, and Özal was famously quoted as saying that "a single violation of the constitution would not harm anyone." It is but one more example of nepotism and self-interested, unethical behavior that has unfortunately only worsened over time, rather than the reverse.

After the establishment of the first private TV channels, Magic Box (now Star TV) and Teleon, private radio stations also entered the market. People immediately embraced diversity, and when private radio was banned for a while in the summer of 1993, black ribbons were tied to car antennas in protest. CDs were available, but they were expensive, and cassette tapes were still widely popular. I remember listening to new-generation pop stars on cassettes.

The media in Türkiye have never been fully free. Official government censorship, as well as self-censorship to avoid displeasing the ruler, have been part of the landscape for journalists and publishers dating back to the Ottoman period. The government had a legal right to control the press. Opposition publications were frequently closed, and violators were often imprisoned or exiled. Though the laws have been revised over time and enforcement has varied, the profession has always been difficult in Türkiye and "insulting" or questioning secularism or the government, the role of the military in politics, minority rights, and other sensitive topics has risked reprisal. Numerous journalists have been attacked, jailed, and even murdered.

Yet there used to be some room for the media to be critical or parody society, including the president and his family, for example, which is inconceivable today. Recent actions have brought the status of press freedom to a new low. Most of the major outlets are owned or controlled by the government or companies close to Erdoğan.

There are a few other outlets that manage to survive, but they are under constant threat and have largely adopted the government narrative on the July 15, 2016 coup attempt, for example, despite claims of independence. Fines and other punitive measures are commonplace for any outlet or individual that is deemed to be critical of the government using extremely broad and arbitrary parameters that severely limit the ability to practice true journalism.

There are numerous examples of the use of pressure tactics, legislation, and arrest to intimidate and control information. A law passed in 2022 calls for up to four to five years' imprisonment for stories and online posts that "spread information that is inaccurate" designed to "create fear and panic" or "disrupt Turkey's domestic and external security," "public order," or "public health."

I have never considered my family to be particularly political. They were as interested in politics as anyone else, but I think I was a somewhat atypical girl to have developed a passionate interest in politics very early in life.

After Özal's election to the presidency, the ANAP party he founded was led by a young, Western-educated, liberal-minded man named Mesut Yılmaz. The elections of October 20, 1991 were the first national elections that I followed closely with great excitement. While my peers were interested in pop stars and actors and spoke of boys and romance, I had a large poster of Yılmaz hanging in my room throughout my middle school years. In retrospect, this sounds strange, even to me. I do not know why politicians appealed to me rather than the more typical sources of interest to young girls.

By the time I was 14, I had become a news and politics junkie. In a way, I guess journalism has always been in my blood, though it took me time to come to it as a profession. A childhood friend, Şebnem, and I created a small newspaper that reported the news in our apartment complex. I remember that one neighbor we interviewed was not happy with our headline, but I guess that was good preparation for my future career.

I was somewhat precocious. I even wrote a letter to Chelsea Clinton when Bill Clinton was elected to the U.S.

presidency. I was intrigued by a peer who was the "first daughter." I handwrote the letter in poor English, photocopied it, and sent four duplicates just to make sure that Chelsea received it. Some months later, the arrival of two envelopes with the White House logo sent our whole apartment building into a frenzy. "Sevgi received correspondence from the White House!" was repeated with astonishment many times among our neighbors.

My parents did not go to any lengths to encourage me to be especially curious or interested in politics. On the contrary, after this courtesy reply from the White House, my father drily commented that my uncle Hüseyin also did such "strange things," remarking that he had sent a letter to Diana, Princess of Wales, when she was a very popular figure in the 1980s. My father is a very practical person and viewed such activities as pointless. Now, as an adult who had to struggle to survive in exile, I can understand why he focused on earning a living and recommended that I take up a profession where I could "sign documents" instead of studying the humanities, but at the time, I was not dissuaded in the least.

My admiration for Yılmaz became almost an obsession. I collected news clippings about him and dutifully pasted them into albums every day after school. On March 28, 1993, my biggest dream came true. I had the chance to meet Yılmaz when my uncle Hüseyin paged my father to say that he was dining in the same restaurant in Istanbul. Yılmaz, who was not particularly known for friendliness, was not very receptive to the enormous interest of a teenager, but he graciously agreed to a photo and his wife, Berna, was kind enough to give me her fax number and talk with me briefly. I was very excited. When

I wrote down my name and information, the people at the table thought it was cute that my hand was shaking.

With Mesut Yılmaz (far left), March 1993
(I am standing center left)

Less than a month after I met Yılmaz, on April 17, 1993, President Özal died suddenly of a heart attack. To this day, his death remains somewhat suspicious. There was speculation of possible deep state engineering of the fatal event or even foreign interference, and doubts have lingered ever since. Significant investigation, including exhumation of the remains and an autopsy in 2012, has not resolved the uncertainty. First aid had been administered privately at the presidential palace, there were conflicting reports about the initial response, no autopsy was performed at the time, and blood samples were lost.

Over the years, his wife Semra and his son Ahmet have both claimed that Özal was poisoned, but changing statements and theories hurt their credibility. Since Özal had ventured into topics that disturbed some factions and

CHOICES

had survived an earlier assassination attempt, the poisoning claim may have merit. However, when his son began to use Özal's death for his own interests and to blame various actors for his father's death, he and the issue were scorned by many, especially on social media. The final report issued in 2012 found that the body did contain poison, but the cause of death was unclear. It remains yet another of the country's mysteries.

I remember the day Özal died very clearly. One of my middle school teachers, Selami Sekban, had brought me and his son to take the high school entrance exam that Saturday morning in Istanbul's Cağaloğlu neighborhood, a historic quarter also known as the site of the publication of the country's first newspapers. Competition for entry was fierce, and these exams were extremely important. Though there are now more high schools and universities, and the system has changed somewhat, students prepare for years and feel tremendous pressure.

When we left the building after the long exam, Mr. Sekban told us the news that Özal had passed away. He must have been surprised by the grief of a 14-year-old girl in response to the death of a politician. Not only did I cry rivers of tears, but I could not even go to school the following week because I was too sad to leave the house. I watched the remembrances offered by his friends on TV, and some neighbors even visited me to offer their condolences. I was sad not only because of the suddenness of Özal's death, but also because I would never be able to meet him. I wanted to go to the funeral, but my parents would not allow me to attend because of the huge crowd. It was probably one of the most heavily attended funerals in the history of the country and several international leaders were among the attendees.

Özal was one of the most influential political figures in the history of the country. Some loved him, others hated him, depending on their position on the ideological spectrum. His open and deeply held religiosity was important for the conservative majority, but this and some of his efforts to change the status quo were not always well received. He was devout, but in many ways lived a secular lifestyle and applied a Western approach to governance; he maintained a distance from both the hardline secularists and radical branches of Islam. He was pragmatic but had grand goals. He was considered quite liberal compared with his predecessors and was associated with prosperity, but respect and trust were given grudgingly. He was a polarizing figure and legitimate criticism can be made, but without doubt his impact was significant.

After Özal's unexpected death, Türkiye entered another decade marked by unrest, instability, and suspicion about deep state activities. Demirel once again rose to prominence and became president in 1993.

CHAPTER 4

The 1990s were difficult, both politically for the nation and for me personally. I began to feel the angst of adolescence and pondered the meaning of life. I was growing up in a devout family, but our observance was not much more than the preservation of traditional religious practices. In our apartment complex, my family was about the only one that wanted to send their children to religious summer school to learn to read the Quran in its original script. I had learned to read some Arabic as a child after some classes at an all-girls school above a mosque, but as I grew older, I did not like being the only girl in the neighborhood who went to religious school wearing a headscarf even for a few weeks and I soon stopped attending.

I was not pressured to be overtly observant, yet the whole issue of clothing was a big challenge for me, as it probably is for every girl in Türkiye who is a devout Muslim even more so than it ordinarily is for young girls. My peers who grew up in more "modern" families could wear whatever they liked—short shorts, miniskirts, tank tops, etc.—but in my family, there was a limit.

My parents did not expect me to cover my head or wear long skirts and long sleeves like some conservative parents do, but there were some rules, particularly after puberty. I remember arguing with my mother when she was angry with me for buying short shorts, but she allowed longer shorts, which we called "Bermudas." My father also paid close attention to how my first sister and I dressed. I remember that in my early teens they did not permit even sleeveless T-shirts, or the popular Levi's 501 jeans, much to our frustration.

He later became much more liberal, but at the time, we struggled a bit to find a balance we could all be content with. He has become less strict in a number of ways over time as Türkiye changed, like many others. When I was a teenager, he interfered when it came to how his two oldest daughters dressed, but with his younger daughters, he was much more relaxed.

Like any teenager, I was exploring my new status of no longer being a child and beginning to establish my identity. The messages received from the external world are important to this developmental period, which presents both opportunities and vulnerabilities as expectations and personal understanding of the self, environment, and life as a whole take on new significance.

In all, my parents' attitudes toward my upbringing were fairly lenient. I did not have restrictions that some of my peers contended with, such as no sleepovers and no travel outside of the city before the end of high school. I was able to find a midpoint between my desires for freedom and autonomy and my parents' desire for boundaries. They trusted me and gave me latitude.

As it happened, over time I became more religious and adopted their standards to some degree. Once that was established, I was virtually free to do what I liked. Truthfully, I never wanted to do anything that my parents would have been concerned about. Looking back, I somewhat regret not having been at least a bit more daring in my youth, like some of my peers were. On the other hand, since I had essentially only self-imposed limitations, especially once at university, it was probably my nature to always be something of a "good girl." Perhaps, without realizing it, my family and social circle had exerted influence with high expectations and praise for my morals, discipline, and rationality. But I never felt any internal contradiction and simply never thought of rejecting that structure. I was modest and responsible without it being any sort of burden.

I had been free to find my own path without significant objection, but in high school I began to feel the external pressure of illiberal secularism more keenly. In the summer of 1993, I was enrolled in one of the oldest and most highly regarded high schools in Türkiye. I had always been academically successful and a favorite of the teachers; however, Kabataş High School (formerly Kabataş Erkek Lisesi), a boys' school that had recently begun to admit girls, had a resolutely secularist ethos. In the eyes of the teachers, who were proud Kemalists, religion was to be strictly confined to the private sphere since faith was something between God and the individual. I feared discrimination and did not tell anyone but my closest friends that I had begun to observe daily prayer practice.

A fear of sharia, or Islamic law, had been growing in Türkiye, in part in reaction to the Iranian revolution and subsequent fundamentalist rule. Then, an Islamist political party won control of the city government in the two largest cities, Istanbul and Ankara. Anyone who simply wanted to practice Islam could easily have been labeled "reactionary."

In such a climate, I felt uncomfortable because my mother wore a religious headscarf, which was seen by many as a flag of political Islam. My family, and certainly my mother, was never ideological, but appearance mattered, especially for a high school student. I hate to admit it, but I remember feeling anxious when my mother came to school for parent-teacher conferences. My father's indifference to such events was well established, but I wanted him to attend rather than my mother. Sadly, I also remember feeling stressed when I was acknowledged for academic achievement in a presentation on stage in 1997 because my visibly religious mother would also be in the spotlight.

Modesty in clothing for both men and women is prescribed in the Quran, but interpretation regarding a headscarf varies. While some consider it essential, others consider it optional. It is a particularly contentious issue in Türkiye, given the complicated history of the roles of Islam and secularism.

I view it as a personal choice, though the social pressure and emphasis surrounding the use of a headscarf that I experienced in my teenage years doubtless had an impact on me. It carried significant stigma and limitations. At times, I considered adopting the practice, even later in life, but I do not see it as a requirement. I am devout and conscientious in the observance of my faith and do not find it paradoxical that I choose not to cover my head. Equally, I believe that women who choose to cover must be granted that religious freedom without equivocation.

As in many religions, there is a spectrum of opinion and observance.

My parents have always supported my decision, though I suspect that my mother might have preferred it if I wore a headscarf. They understood the restriction it could have on my future, as well as the social impact. Students were often profiled based on their religiosity. I can recall when one junior-high student was accused of wearing a headscarf outside the school and the assistant principal gave her a warning. There was also a concerted campaign against the "dangers" of the faith-based Gülen movement.

Fethullah Gülen is an Islamic cleric and scholar who began to develop a movement known as the Hizmet (service) or Gülen movement in the 1960s as an imam, one who leads prayer. It is a civil society movement that emphasizes compatibility between Islam and modernity. Gülen's teachings recommend embracing science, education, and public service while incorporating spirituality. Gülen has condemned violence and the politicization of religion, and he has expressed the belief that a moderate and flexible alternative approach can help reduce the influence of Islamic extremists. He advocates for interfaith dialogue and has met with leadership from the Vatican and Jewish organizations as part of the effort to promote tolerance and harmony.

As the movement grew, it began to establish schools that eventually numbered well over 1,000 secular educational institutions designed to provide a holistic education of high standards in more than 160 countries, in addition to other support organizations, such as dormitories. The curriculum does not include religion beyond any state requirements; however, teachers and staff are expected to be role models and teach ethical values through example.

The success of the movement led to concern and opposition from both staunch secularists, who viewed it as threatening to the secular regime, and radical Islamists, who considered it too accommodating to Western thought. The structure of the movement is opaque and informal. Supporters are inspired by Gülen, not directed, and while a closed, hierarchical organization was, in part, a measure of protection as well as a reflection of modesty, it added to suspicion of hidden motives and activities. Gülen encouraged sympathizers to enter the state bureaucracy and business community as a means of demonstrating the potential of his teachings, but accusations of subversive activity quickly followed.

Gülen had a relatively good relationship with the government and the military in the 1980s. Özal supported the movement because he approved of Islamic-motivated entrepreneurialism and engagement with the world. This continued into the 1990s, but the sentiment would soon change.

Though the Gülen movement was viewed with misgiving and condescension by many, in my family, the schools run by the movement were well regarded. They were known for their academic standards and success. Students from both secular and religious families attended for that very reason. My uncle Hüseyin had enrolled his son, two years younger than I, in one of the movement's best-known private high schools in Istanbul, Fatih College (Fatih Koleji). There, I saw a different type of teacher.

They were not only highly educated and dedicated, but also paid great attention to the students. I was really surprised when I first heard that the teachers made home visits to each student and developed personal mentoring relationships. This service continued even beyond high school and was genuinely helpful, but it was also part of their effort to win the hearts of students and generate sympathy for the Gülen movement.

When my father suggested that I enroll in the girls' branch of Fatih College, I declined, despite the proven quality of the education, perhaps because of the stigma attached to the Gülen movement. I had followed politics closely enough to sense that profiling could be a problem and I did not want to be labeled by going to a Gülenist school. I also felt that the girls' school would not be given as much importance as the boys' school. Unfortunately, I believe I was correct in that concern. Instead, I chose Kabataş High School, which had a good reputation, and as a bonus, offered a wonderful view of the Bosphorus. I have never regretted my decision, despite experiencing some social pressure at school.

Because the university entrance exams are also extremely competitive, many students attend preparatory classes to augment their standard education. Initially, I attended a secular prep school, but I was dissatisfied with the administration's laxity, and I felt that I would be better served at a Gülenist preparatory school, FEM (Fırat Eğitim Merkezi). Based on the results of an entrance test, FEM waived my tuition, but the cost was not my first priority. At the beginning of my last year at Kabataş, an assistant principal called me to her office and asked me which prep school I wanted to attend. When I said FEM, she asked me why. To avoid judgment, I mentioned the tuition exemption. She countered that the prep school I had tried before was willing to offer scholarships to the top students of our high school. I do not remember exactly how I responded, but this anecdote illustrates the deliberate attempt to encourage students to avoid the Gülenists.

Türkan Saylan, a medical doctor, academic, and social activist who was known for her resolute secular activism and giving scholarships to needy girls in rural areas, paid regular visits to Kabataş High School. On one occasion, Saylan held a conference for parents. My father attended and told me that Saylan had advised parents not to send their children to preparatory courses run by the Gülen movement, implying that it was somehow unwise and risky. My father said that he told Saylan she could not tell them where to send their children. I was a bit worried about the reaction to this at school, but there were no repercussions beyond the frequent general warnings about the Gülenists.

Aside from the disapproval of religiosity, I was happy at Kabataş High School. I had the impression that, despite some old and eccentric teachers, the school was worthy of its good reputation and that the students were hardworking and ambitious. I was lucky enough to have an English teacher who was something like a Turkish version of the Robin Williams character in the film *Dead Poets Society*. İbrahim Yücel was different from other teachers. He not only helped us love English as a foreign language, but he also had a much more relaxed attitude than other instructors.

I remember that a classmate once sat on the lectern instead of a chair during class. Any other teacher would have punished such behavior. In Türkiye, students typically stood when the teacher entered the room as an important sign of respect. Yücel explained to us that respect has nothing to do with how we greet him, but rather with how we thought about him.

June 1997

I had some other great teachers in high school, but because of their advanced age and peculiar habits, at least in the eyes of teenagers, we had a lot of fun imitating them and laughing. I enjoyed the jokes, conversations, and walks we had near the Bosphorus Bridge during long lunch breaks, despite being a bit more somber and worried than your average teenager.

I was very interested in politics and paid no attention to boys at school. My classmates generally seemed childish to me, and I was probably too serious in their view. After all, how many high school students would take a cab instead of the school bus in order to get home in time for budget debates in parliament? Looking back, I do not remember having a crush on anyone until the middle of my university education, which seems somewhat odd to me now. I was too busy worrying about the future of my country and only paid attention to "important people."

CHAPTER 5

It was March 1994 when there was a strong resurgence of political Islam in big cities with the election of Recep Tayyip Erdoğan to be the mayor of Istanbul. My family and I were never Islamists, and though I, too, initially had some misgivings, when people spoke out against Erdoğan because of his religious identity, I was frustrated. Although he was only an elected mayor, I recall that women in our apartment complex feared the introduction of sharia law and impositions such as separate buses for women.

These fears seemed unfounded and excessive to me. The fierce and pre-emptive reaction may have contributed to people like me overlooking some of Erdoğan's early anti-democratic statements. In retrospect, I agree that one should always be suspicious when a politician, regardless of popular support, publicly says that democracy is like a train that you get off once you reach your desired destination. But it is important to remember that in the early years he appeared to be reasonable.

His performance seemed to prove pessimists wrong. There was no doubt that he was an influential public speaker who had significant appeal to the religious majority and those disillusioned with the mismanagement and corruption of other parties. Many people saw

Erdoğan as "one of them" because he had grown up in the working-class Istanbul neighborhood of Kasımpaşa, where many felt like outsiders. Fears of religious rule seemed to have been groundless, and in fact, Erdoğan gained more popular support as municipality services improved. For example, garbage was picked up on time, the important Golden Horn estuary of the Bosphorus was cleaned and no longer gave off a rank odor, and natural gas began to replace coal, which improved the problem of air pollution in the city.

This last change was a positive development for the city, but it was a difficult adjustment for my family's business. The coal plant had to be relocated outside of Istanbul because Mayor Erdoğan banned coal processing and the sale of domestic coal within the city limits. My family decided to open an office in the industrial city of Gebze, just outside Istanbul, and focus on importing coal that was of better quality. Domestic coal was cheap but lower in calorific value than other types of coal and resulted in more pollution. Their income probably decreased, but I welcomed the decision as benefiting the common good.

I suspect that only a few in his inner circle knew that Erdoğan likely began to build his own personal treasury starting in the 1990s. When I was a journalist years later, in the wake of corruption investigations, a columnist close to Islamist circles told us in an editorial meeting that he had seen suitcases full of cash brought into the municipality. Yet, even after there was significant evidence of corruption, many who are enamored of Erdoğan continue to defend him, arguing that despite his theft, he gives more to the people than anyone previously in office.

CHOICES

In my early teens I was searching for meaning and explanations, and in August 1994, I was quite shaken by the death of a young journalist, Hande Mumcu, and her fiancé in a car accident. The story was in the headlines for days, perhaps because she had previously been involved in a political scandal and there may have been suspicions about the circumstances of the crash, though I do not recall being aware of that. I think the possibility of death at a young age must have frightened me. Coupled with my pre-existing ontological thoughts and concerns, I was led to seek refuge in God.

That summer, I began to pray as much as I could. I would still go to the beach and have fun with my friends, but I would return home when it was time to pray. When it came time to make a choice between the two, I chose my responsibility to the Creator. In that sense, no one forced me to be devout, but my choices were shaped to some extent by the increasing polarization and strict lines in the country during my teenage years.

Although I had no negative prejudices against the Gülen movement, I was probably influenced by the general cautious attitude toward it, so when I started attending the Beşiktaş branch of FEM, I did not even want them to know that I was already incorporating daily prayer and other religious duties into my life. The prep school did not have a religious curriculum, but it was a conservative environment with visibly observant teachers and staff. I remember not praying at school for the first few weeks and making up for it at home. It may seem incongruous, but I did not want them to think I was insincere and only trying to look like one of them or curry favor by acting religious. The entire subject of faith was fraught with potential risk and repercussions, and my younger self struggled with how to manage this atmosphere.

It was difficult to accommodate religious practices into a standard lifestyle. Secularists often claim that piety was not restricted, but that was not the case. Atatürk never forbade the headscarf, but very actively discouraged its use in public venues, and after the 1980 coup, it was formally banned in public institutions, including universities. The ban was not always enforced however, which at first allowed many devout women to graduate, but it would soon become a very high-profile and contentious issue.

Societal discrimination and government pressure made life difficult in general society for those who were religiously observant, even if it was not visible (such as wearing a headscarf). I had learned at a young age to keep my religiosity as discreet as possible without being told to do so by anyone, as many wrongly assume. At the time, I guess I was afraid of being left out of secular circles if they knew that I prayed five times a day and did not consume alcohol. I wanted people to know me as a person rather than judging me based on my religious identity.

Unfortunately, the role of religion in society continues to be a fault line in Türkiye, abused by both ardent secularists and political Islamists. I increasingly believe that religious practice is a bond between God and the individual and therefore advocate for a liberal form of passive secularism in which the state remains neutral toward all faiths and ensures freedom to worship or not, as desired. Thus far, we have only seen the pendulum swing from one extreme that severely limited religiosity to the other extreme that imposed its understanding of the importance of religion. I reject both approaches; individuals should be free to practice their faith as they wish.

One day, one of the philosophy teachers at Kabataş, Ms. Aliye, saw me and a few classmates going to FEM. "Do not go if they invite you to their houses," she said, in an open admonition. She was likely referring to the student housing for which the Gülen movement was known. Students of the prep schools (dershane) were sometimes housed in proprietary residences for only a modest fee with the expectation that they would observe certain rules and habits, such as attending daily informal discussion meetings, not staying out late, and other conduct that conformed with an Islamic lifestyle and the teachings of the movement. For many families, this conservative environment was viewed as safe, and families, those from less urban areas in particular, often preferred this kind of student housing.

Promising students were sometimes asked to help in class, invited to supporters' homes, or to attend group study sessions. After a few months at FEM, I was invited to a dershane house in Beşiktaş for additional study time in preparation for the university placement exams. Only a small percentage of the millions of students who take the exams receive a university placement. Therefore, extra classes and rigorous study are very common. The pressure on students is enormous, despite various changes to the system to increase access. Equity is also questionable, considering the cost of private prep classes and tutoring.

I was aware that the invitation was not just to learn but to introduce myself to the movement. It would be an environment infused with Islamic habits and the community's ideals of service, but I did not mind. I knew that these were decent people and I was not concerned. There was absolutely no pressure to do anything other than to work hard.

During my final year of high school, I spent most of my Friday nights at the dershane and attended FEM on the weekends. All we did was study with older "sisters" who were university students, ask them for tips on how to succeed in the exams, and sometimes just talk and laugh, like any other teenagers. Despite the significant stress of life-determining exams and worries about the future, we also found time to laugh about the smallest and silliest things. Sometimes I miss those days that, while very challenging, were more carefree than I realized.

Gülen was inspired by Said Nursi, the revered founder of the worldwide Nurcu movement named after him. Nursi was a Kurdish Muslim scholar who was born during the latter part Ottoman Empire and faced resistance and persecution from the secular regime until his death in 1960. He was a devout Muslim who believed that the application of modern science and logic were necessary components of a successful future. He advocated for a reinterpretation of Islam according to the needs of modern society.

I first became acquainted with his books at the dershane, when I was 17 or 18 years old. On one weekend at a dershane house, a group of students read a chapter from Nursi's well-known collection, *Risale-i Nur* (Epistles of Light). I sat with them and listened. I still remember the subject of that meeting: the importance of daily prayers. What was new, at least compared with other religious texts, was a narrative that appealed not only to the heart, but also to the mind. The chapter we discussed contained a famous analogy between investing a gold coin and investing in your eternal life. The 24 hours of a day are like 24 coins in your pocket. If you invest one rather than spend it, you have made a wise decision.

I was already inclined to turn to something greater in the face of life's challenges and I prayed regularly, but Nursi's teachings combined with the open-minded approach of the Gülen movement seemed like a reasonable "third way." In a sense, it offered the best of both worlds for someone who did not fit in with either oppressive secularism or political Islamism. Looking at these bright, devout students at prestigious universities, I was reassured that it was indeed possible to be both modern and religious.

I had long wanted to study political science. Until I started at FEM, my goal was to be accepted into the nation's oldest faculty of political science, often referred to by its old name of Mülkiye (civil service), but it was no longer the elite institution it once was. Top grades were no longer required for entry, and moreover, the language of instruction was Turkish in a world where English had become indispensable for career advancement.

A key difference between the Gülen-inspired prep schools and others was that they really expressed an active interest in the future of the students. This included providing intensive mentoring. I had felt uncertain about scoring well enough on the placement exam, even though I was well above the national average, but thanks to intensive math support from FEM, some private tutoring, and hard work, I was able to make tremendous progress within a few months. I scored 106th in the social sciences segment among the more than 1 million students who took the national placement exam.

Years of hard work had paid off, and with the typical, limited scope of a teenager, I felt like I had overcome the biggest obstacle in life. With the encouragement of Ms. Fatma, a tutor and older "sister" at FEM and a student at Boğaziçi, I set my sights higher and aimed for the Ivy League of Türkiye, selecting Bilkent University and Boğaziçi University as my ranked choices.

Personal trauma in my family also contributed to the strains of this period and a certain distraction and withdrawal from following political events as closely as usual during my senior year of high school. One day in 1996, my uncle Mehmet was murdered in his office. He was only 35. Shock and grief upset my stomach and my mood for weeks, if not months.

I think perhaps I had a special place in his heart as the first child of the next generation in the family, and he definitely had a special place in my heart. Unlike my father, Mehmet was generous in showing us his love. It is an often-told family anecdote that when I was little and Uncle Mehmet left to perform his mandatory military service, I had wished that my father would go to the army instead of my beloved uncle.

To this day, I do not know why my uncle was killed. It seems it may have been related to a financial dispute, but I cannot be certain. I wanted to go to the trial of his murderer, but my father did not allow it. The story was sensationalized in the news, and my classmates asked me a lot of questions, but I had few answers. My family was better off than some around us, but my uncle had led a truly luxurious life. I had been with him at Akmerkez, the first upscale shopping mall in Istanbul, and had seen him spend money lavishly. In contrast to his upbringing, he did not live a conservative lifestyle. He loved nightlife and always seemed to have a new girlfriend after a brief, failed marriage that haunted him and the family for decades.

I knew about my uncle's ambition to become very wealthy and that he had admired and been friends with Bekir Kutmangil, a rich businessman in the mining sector who was also murdered, not long before my uncle suffered the same fate. The business environment at the time was not clearly regulated and boundaries were murky. This may have been a contributing factor to my uncle's death. I remember that my grandparents feared for their remaining sons afterwards, and that they received threatening phone calls. I do not know who might have threatened them or why, but I recall being extremely concerned about my family's well-being.

I was just a high school student in the 1990s and preoccupied with my own small world, but the generally depressing climate in the country was inescapable. Economic instability arose once again when short-term populist measures to boost economic growth without addressing underlying flaws quickly failed. A series of weak coalition governments could not curb a deteriorating situation.

Mesut Yılmaz, Tansu Çiller, and Necmettin Erbakan, rivals but coalition partners when necessary, all held office as prime minister for brief periods of time in the early to mid-1990s in a dizzying series of alliances, but they were unable to maintain control or resolve economic instability. Çiller, a center-right politician who was celebrated as the country's first female prime minister, was a modern, well-educated economist and secularist. She is notable as one of the few women who reached the heights of power in Turkish politics. Interestingly, her husband, Özer Uçuran, took her last name, which is very unusual in Türkiye, even for today's generation. However, she was dogged by allegations of corruption. In part to escape investigation and hearings, she abandoned a partnership with the more ideologically similar Yılmaz and formed an unlikely alliance with Erbakan, head of the Welfare Party (RP), a political Islamist movement.

One of the accusations Çiller faced was related to the use of the prime minister's discretionary fund. This account is often used for special intelligence operations and other purposes that justifiably are not made public, but she refused to explain large expenditures, even to President Demirel or to her successor as prime minister. Later revelations suggest that it may well have funded efforts to destroy the PKK and involved links to drug trafficking and organized crime.

An escalation in bloody clashes between the state and the Kurdish movement, mysterious arrests, torture, and murders of Kurdish civilians, as well as enforced disappearances of suspected sympathizers of PKK members carried out by security forces, police, or their proxies in what became famous white Renault vehicles were commonplace, though routinely denied by authorities and largely unreported in the censored media. Conservative estimates of the number killed or disappeared number several thousand. There was a climate of fear, anger, and turmoil.

A traffic accident in November 1996, some 100 miles outside of Istanbul in the town of Susurluk, would prove to be a tipping point. A truck rear-ended a car, killing three occupants of the car and seriously injuring the fourth. Their identities revealed collaboration and illegal state activity that rocked the country and exposed the deep state. Shock waves continue to resonate to this day.

A police chief who had been an investigator of organized crime and a leader of an anti-terrorism unit; an ultranationalist assassin and heroin smuggler with an international reputation who was working for the state intelligence service; and a former beauty queen, the mistress of the hitman, were killed in the crash. The fourth occupant of the car was a Kurdish leader and politician who was a member of a pro-government militia and was working undercover for the state against the PKK.

Weapons and false identification documents found in the vehicle made protestations of innocent coincidence exceedingly implausible. The accident unmasked a state that was indeed complicit in both extrajudicial killings and drug trafficking. The disclosure of a network and alliance of the local mafia and the state led to public outrage. Protests were held to demand clean politics, including civic moments such as residents turning off the lights for one minute every evening.

There were several investigations, but ultimately little accountability and details remain obscure, but this incident had effects that continue to be felt. Trust in leadership was further eroded and an already-present willingness to believe that covert conspiracies of the powerful were threatening society were strengthened. The truth was almost certainly more complex than a single, centralized organization, but the fact that criminal acts had been endorsed and orchestrated was undeniable.

Erbakan, prime minister in 1996, had been a leader in Islamist political activity for many years, but successive efforts were banned for violating the constitutional separation of religion and state. The National View (or Vision) (Milli Görüş) espoused by Erbakan emphasized the moral and spiritual strength of Islam and rejected Western values, instead favoring ties with Muslim countries as a preferred means to advance development and economic independence. He had been able to increase the voter base for his party in the 1990s, but their vote share and subsequent power following the 1995 election was a surprise.

I had an informal meeting with Erbakan in the summer of 1994 when my family was returning home from a vacation on the Aegean coast and we stopped in the resort town of Altınoluk in northwestern Türkiye to visit neighbors who were spending the summer there. It was public knowledge that Erbakan had a summer home in the area. Out of sheer curiosity, I wanted to pay him a visit.

When I approached the house, I could see Erbakan sitting in the garden, just off the secluded beach. Of course, the security guards at the gate did not take a request from a 15-year-old seriously, but I indicated that I would not mind waiting. Erbakan must have wondered what I wanted because he started talking to me from a distance. I said that I would like to talk with him, and I asked him if his daughter's wedding at a posh hotel would alienate his conservative supporters as some had claimed, just like a journalist.

Erbakan, who surely had not expected such a serious question from a teenager, seemed impressed and invited me in. I told him quite frankly that I was a supporter of Turgut Özal and had no interest in the RP. Nonetheless, he was kind enough to talk with me for more than two hours. Though he explained why his idea of a "just order" based on Islamic principles was much better than that presented by Özal, I was not convinced. Erbakan's dreams seemed, even to me, to be unrealistic.

When he finally came to power in 1996, he was confronted with realpolitik and was unable to implement his utopian goals, such as an interest-free economy. His overtures to Arab nations were unsuccessful and he also failed to appreciate the popular indignation and anger following the Susurluk scandal. His popularity declined, and critically, his reforms to enhance the influence of Islam in society and concepts such as an Islamic security organization to rival NATO and an Islamic currency had greatly worried the secular establishment.

With Erbakan (far right) at his summer home, 1994

The powerful military had been watching closely and issued warnings to the government about the direction of the country. With the assistance of members of the media and other groups, the National Security Council began to stoke pre-existing fears of Islamic fundamentalism. Voices of opposition were intimidated and punished. This perceived Islamic menace had replaced communism as the existential global threat in the years after the Cold War and the more recent war against the PKK, which was in retreat by the mid-1990s. Numerous examples of the rise of a "reactionary" movement promoted by the Islamist government were offered to reinforce the aversion of many secularists to anything visibly religious. The Erbakan government did nothing to ease tensions, and the prime minister is said to have not taken the threat seriously.

On February 28, 1997, the National Security Council launched what has been called a "postmodern coup." No blood was shed, the military did not suspend parliament or the constitution, but the coup was nonetheless brutal. A memorandum containing 18 resolutions with actions needed to protect secularism was issued to the government. It was, in effect, an ultimatum, and Erbakan was subsequently forced to resign, despite agreeing to the memorandum measures. The demands limited religious expression in a number of ways, including firm enforcement of a ban on the use of a headscarf in the public sector, which included universities as well as all state offices. An elected member of parliament was denied the ability to take the oath of office in 1999 because she wore a headscarf. It was a painful issue for many pious women, excluding them from education, employment, and full participation in society. The ban remained in place until 2013.

The 1997 coup also changed the life of Fethullah Gülen. He had not openly supported Erbakan, choosing to maintain distance from political Islamism. However, as anti-religious fervor grew, Gülen was also implicated and charged with anti-secular activities. Gülen left Türkiye in 1999 and lives in Pennsylvania.

Additional social, political, and economic disruption followed, and the lasting effects of the "coup by memorandum" continue to this day. While bloodless, the events were engraved into the collective political Islamist psyche in Türkiye and contributed to the environment of today in many ways, including the formation of the party of the current government.

Just after I graduated from high school, my father gave me and my first sister a great gift. Her school had organized a trip to California, and in the summer of 1997, we spent three wonderful weeks in the Los Angeles area, a completely new experience for us. Having grown up watching popular American TV series and Hollywood movies, it was like a dream come true to visit the U.S. as a teenager, especially sights like Universal Studios, Disneyland, Bel Air, and Rodeo Drive. I fell in love with the U.S. during that trip, despite the fact that violent images from films also made us feel somewhat nervous occasionally. At that time, I could only dream of perhaps studying there someday. In hindsight, I wish I had had some mentors who encouraged me to pursue even an undergraduate degree in the U.S. Who knows what direction my life could have taken?

CHAPTER 6

In a country like Türkiye, where people are almost forced to align themselves with a social or ideological camp, the Gülen movement was perhaps the inevitable path for someone like me, especially after I left Istanbul to study at Bilkent University. I was thrilled to be admitted to a school like Bilkent, but the campus is located in the heartland of Anatolia, in the capital city of Ankara, which is considered a dull city by almost everyone from Istanbul, the more cosmopolitan, social and financial capital of the country. I now wonder about my decision to leave Istanbul, but at the time it was exciting.

A few days before enrollment began in September 1997, the whole world was shocked by the sudden death of Diana, Princess of Wales, first wife of King Charles III and mother of Princes William and Harry, who died in a controversial car accident with her Muslim boyfriend in Paris. She was a popular icon for her glamor and activism, as well as her difficult story as a member of the British royal family, but to this day, I do not understand why her death shook me so. This was a worldwide phenomenon, but still somewhat surprising. Despite my excitement about university, I was so saddened by her death that I remember being affected for the whole drive from Istanbul to Ankara with my parents, one of my sisters, and a classmate, Ayşegül.

The start of university study for anyone fresh out of high school is like entering a new universe, but in Türkiye it is an even more abrupt change. Education is, or at least was, conducted with an almost military discipline. As just one example, from elementary school through high school, uniforms were mandatory throughout the country. In my childhood, the uniforms were black. I suppose this was a practical consideration, but it seems a bit odd. In middle school and high school, my uniforms were also in somber colors, like dark blue and gray. The school uniforms were, as in the military, part of an effort to standardize and homogenize, creating literal uniformity. In addition to perhaps attempting to minimize social differences for the benefit of the students, this was consistent with years of indoctrination intended to promote notions of identity that did not deviate from the approved, at least in terms of certain themes such as the unity of the nation and the worship of Atatürk. University represented completely new territory.

Thanks to the efforts of Gülen movement sympathizers, I was able to make friends at Bilkent even before I arrived. A friend of a friend from FEM found me in Istanbul after I was admitted to Bilkent and met me and my parents on campus. My parents were relieved to see that their teenaged daughter was friends with respectable and reliable people. I was the first girl in my family to go to another city to study. In this, my father was quite progressive compared with his peers and given his conservative background. I could not even imagine telling my father about something like a boyfriend, but I also never feared that he would reject or deny me my dreams.

SEVGİ AKARÇEŞME

I went to Ankara with a great deal of enthusiasm and idealism. As a political junkie, I wanted to do all kinds of internships in the nation's capital, but Ankara disappointed me very early on. Bilkent seemed to be almost disconnected from the rest of the country. Relatively speaking, Bilkent was a liberal campus, but largely apolitical. Students were free to wear whatever they wanted, including the religious headscarf, which was banned at other universities. Following the violence and turmoil seen on campuses in the 1970s and the repression following the 1980 military coup, universities were deliberately made less political.

The fact that Bilkent was as American a campus as possible in the center of Türkiye helped me to nurture a dream of studying in the U.S. Bilkent was a top school for the best students, but also a popular choice for the children of the wealthy from Anatolia and the country's capital who did not necessarily meet the same academic standards. There was a clear gap in the academic level and motivation of some students, at least in departments like mine. Unfortunately, in my opinion, the undergraduate courses in the social sciences were not all that they could have been.

Perhaps it is because I am from Istanbul, but I have always wondered what it would have been like had I elected to study at Boğaziçi University instead, another very highly ranked institution where the student body is more academically homogeneous. On the other hand, at Bilkent I was able to grow and enjoy different benefits away from home at a highly regarded private college with a luxurious campus.

Though there was some student activism at some other universities, the majority of the faculty and students at Bilkent appeared to be focused either on serious academic work or merely the social experience. I remember some male students who came to class with only their cell phone and car keys, no books or study materials of any kind. Many girls came to early morning classes with heavy makeup and carefully coiffed hair and appeared to be similarly unconcerned with their education. I was dedicated to my studies, and while it may not have been the best idea not to mingle more with others, I did not much care that some of us were socially isolated as nerds.

I was unprepared for homesickness. I always thought studying in another city would not only help me become more independent, but also help me escape my parents' unhappy marriage. I only had a teenager's awareness of the complexities, but it was something that troubled me. In addition to other concerns and stresses, as in many families, in-laws were always a source of pressure, and my father's extramarital affair shook the entire family. This is a subject that is still uncomfortable, and it has been something of an elephant in the room since I was young. It took years for me to heal my "father wound," recognizing and understanding human imperfections and their effects.

Yet with the benefit of maturity and experience, I now realize that I lived in a reasonably protected environment with decent people around me. Despite their human shortcomings, my family was honest and good and did their best to meet trying circumstances. Among other things, I learned early to respect the rights of others and the value of integrity. I truly appreciate the comfort zone my parents offered me.

The late 1990s were significantly marked by a new era of tension after the postmodern military coup attempt. The religious, especially but not exclusively the political Islamists, were suppressed, while the secularists, who considered themselves the true owners and guardians of the country, "protected" the republic from the "reactionaries" (Islamists). The oxygen for politics was limited to certain groups.

However, when Abdullah Öcalan, the leader of the outlawed PKK, was captured in 1999 with the help of U.S. intelligence, almost the entire nation rallied around the flag. The hatred of Öcalan was one of the few unifying factors in otherwise fragmented politics.

The Kurds have long suffered under the oppressive policies of the Turkish state and in the greater region. Kurdish citizens of Türkiye were deprived of equal rights unless they agreed to assimilation. The conflict became very complicated, and continues to this day, despite various lulls and attempts at reconciliation over the years. For the overwhelming majority of Turks, Öcalan is a murderer, yet for a significant number of Kurds, he is their leader. After his arrest, the trials made headlines for weeks; the families of fallen soldiers attended, and emotions ran high. Unsurprisingly, Öcalan was sentenced to death, but when Türkiye abolished the death penalty in line with European Union reforms, his sentence was commuted to life imprisonment, and he currently resides in a facility on a small island near the coastline of Istanbul.

CHOICES

Öcalan's sentencing and a flare-up of nationalist sentiment led to a surprise election victory for the veteran social-democrat politician Bülent Ecevit. In Türkiye, universities have historically been predominantly leftist. Bilkent University was one of the least political universities in the country; however, the Nationalist Movement Party (MHP) had a visible and active youth group.

One day, a fellow student suggested that we visit the grave of a founding leader of the MHP, Alparslan Türkeş, who died in April 1997. I never found ideology based on specific identities reasonable, but I went anyway, though I felt a bit uncomfortable. I guess there has always been a curious journalist in me, but today, I would not visit a politician's grave other than for research purposes.

Nationalists in Türkiye often tend to think that they are religious without realizing how much nationalism contradicts the teachings of the Prophet Muhammad. Islam is very communal, despite having schisms and differing interpretations. I was taught that national origin did not confer any sort of superiority or inferiority to others; what matters is one's closeness to God. For many in Türkiye, Islam is part of their Turkish identity and more than a religion. It is complicated for reasons both institutional and personal, and it can be truly difficult to draw definitive lines.

Many have a Muslim cultural identity without being religious. As in numerous countries, faith has become part of the national character, though each individual may or may not hold the beliefs of the predominant religion, and it has a unique weight in each country. In Türkiye, it is particularly complex as a result of history and the role of religion in governance. For example, secularists and atheists are typically still buried according to Muslim tradition in state-supported ceremonies and cemeteries. Though there were exceptions, people tended to socialize with others from their own ideological tribe. This was also true even at Bilkent. Those who did not drink alcohol due to religious concerns were easily labeled and socially segregated. As a result, the optimum social circle for me was peers close to the Gülen movement. They were academically ambitious and had a compatible lifestyle. Today, a reverse in the power dynamic has created a similarly narrow tolerance for the "other," but it is the pious who dominate.

Because social circles were largely divided due to mutual prejudice, fear, ignorance, or simply habit, it was difficult for me, a devout Muslim, to form close friendships with others on campus. Sensitivities to any public display of religion were particularly high and so I did not even think of openly showing my religiosity while at Bilkent. Praying regularly was an indispensable part of my life, and I had concerns about the potential impact it might have, even though it was one of the most Westernized universities in the country. I chose to keep my faith to myself, but since I used a communal bathroom in the dorm, the ritual of cleansing the body before prayer (wudu) was always a problem. I was nervous about my image in the eyes of my classmates and tried to perform it as privately as possible.

Some of the professors seemed to make their disdain for religion clear. One apparently purposely scheduled an exam at the time of breaking the daily fast during the holy month of Ramadan (Ramazan), a period of abstention and reflection when Muslims perform several acts of devotion and gratitude, including refraining from food and drink during daylight hours. Scheduling an exam at this time was particularly difficult for those who observed this fundamental practice of Islam.

Another professor, one who did not ordinarily come to class with a drink, brought a fragrant coffee to the lecture hall during Ramadan. While these examples may perhaps have been unintentional, it did not feel like it. Based on my own and others' experiences, there is no doubt that people are capable of such petty cruelties or that there was an atmosphere of both subtle and not-so-subtle social pressure that was not only permitted but encouraged by some. At the very least, to me it suggests a lack of sensitivity or awareness of students who chose to observe their faith.

The majority of my friends were conservative and pious, and while dating was not openly discussed, most of my closest female friends had dated and formed long-term relationships by the end of university. This was the time it was typically expected to form a permanent attachment. Some who were more committed to the Gülen movement than I seemed to have an easier time. Older "sisters" in the movement often arranged for compatible young people to meet, especially in their last year of study or shortly after graduation.

As far as I observed, these were not arranged marriages and were based entirely on consent, but the movement did want to help like-minded people start families. I was unusually alone for a conservative young woman both in Türkiye and later when I went abroad, and I often complained that I was stuck between two worlds.

I was not completely conservative and traditional, but neither was I completely liberal in terms of my lifestyle. Consequently, I did not fit neatly into any fixed identity. I was a successful young woman with modern ideas and interests, but I had still felt like an outsider from the time I was young due to my faith. Generally, my professors liked me because I worked hard and demonstrated interest, commitment, and integrity. If they came to suspect my religious devotion, they were probably surprised and likely felt sorry for a bright student who they would say was lost to the lure of religion. After all, Islam is still considered backward by many secularists, especially with regard to the position of women. Islam continues to be largely misunderstood in non-Muslim communities and too often misused where it is dominant. While some criticism is legitimate due to the genuinely miserable state of many Muslim societies, this is often more a reflection of authoritarianism. Excessive fear and condemnation of the religion is unfair, unproductive, and very unfortunate, as with any other religion or set of beliefs.

I have to admit that I was as atypical at university as I was in high school. I was intrigued by science and the internet, and I did not even have a romantic crush on anyone until my sophomore year. My interest in politics had long been perceived as a bit odd and too masculine. Though I felt some pressure related to typical expectations regarding marriage, I resisted. I was shy about dating, and I started to experience more self-doubt.

At that time, the internet was not yet accessible everywhere in Türkiye and a high-speed connection was a luxury. At Bilkent, we were able to enjoy the benefits of the online world and I found companionship there. Compared with today's environment, it was very limited, but chat rooms in mIRC, an internet relay chat system, and private instant messaging programs like ICQ were extremely popular.

That was how I met Thomas, a successful young German manager who lived in Istanbul, during my senior year. Shortly after we began to talk online, we arranged to meet in person in Istanbul's posh Bebek neighborhood. He had so many qualities that appealed to me: Cambridge and Wharton educated, confident, well-traveled, and interesting.

He loved extreme sports, which I was not interested in, but he was different and quite charming. He was 15 years older than I and a non-Muslim, but it did not take long for me to fall in love with him. It soon became clear that this would be a platonic and one-sided love; however, that did not prevent the heartbreak of an unrequited first love. Thomas told me that we could only be friends, but he did not disengage. He became almost a mentor to me, and we continued to meet occasionally as friends until he had to return to Germany in the summer of 2001. In retrospect, I think my attitude at the time was a bit immature and naive, but it was a genuine first love.

In August 1999, a devastating earthquake struck the Marmara region, which includes Istanbul, the country's industrial center. My family was safe, but I remember the fear and I cried for days when I saw the rubble and tens of thousands of victims lost to poorly constructed buildings. The public was confronted with a bitter reality: The government had not adequately protected their welfare and was extremely inefficient in its response to the disaster. Just a few months later, there was another earthquake in nearby Düzce. While there were efforts to rebuild and mitigate the risks of future seismic activity, the lack of trust was not repaired. There was damage to more than wood and concrete structures. This would prove to be a recurring problem.

When I graduated third in my class in 2001, one of my dreams came true. I had spent my entire senior year applying to graduate schools in the U.S. almost randomly, based on hearsay and online information, which was still fairly limited at the time. I was convinced that I wanted to get a Ph.D. in the U.S. and I was thrilled to be accepted to a master's and doctorate degree program in political science at the University of Illinois, Chicago.

Bilkent graduation photo, November 2000
(yearbook photo was taken before graduation)

In August of 2001, my father went with me to help get settled in Chicago. I was very excited about starting a new chapter in my life. It seemed achievable, but when I was left alone in a Chicago suburb, I felt like I was stranded on another planet. It was probably the first serious challenge I faced that made me realize that life is not as linear as I had imagined.

In contrast to the California trip and a subsequent trip in 2000 to visit my freshman year roommate, Nuray Tuğrul Yurt, who was pursuing a doctorate with her husband at the University of Arizona, this time I was not in the U.S. for just a short, fun adventure. I was on my own in a strange place again, and it felt different right from the start.

CHAPTER 7

I knew no one in Chicago, except a married Turkish couple I had met through mutual acquaintances in the Gülen movement, İbrahim and Arzu Sayar. İbrahim was a volunteer imam and working to complete his master's degree. It was a joy to learn 17 years later that he became an Islamic chaplain at an Ivy League school in the U.S. Their success with hard work and perseverance is just another example of what the U.S. has to offer immigrants. These friends tried to help me on my own American journey as much as they could with the limited knowledge they had at the time.

Although the university campus was downtown, I rented a one-bedroom apartment in a suburb near O'Hare Airport because İbrahim and Arzu lived there. I found it very difficult to fit into the different environment of graduate school. Homesickness hit me hard once again. To my disappointment, I was not yet ready to study and live on another continent. Everything was different and difficult, from the measurements to the communication style used in daily life.

I knew I liked the overarching system in the U.S., especially because it was meritocratic, but it was too much for me at the time. I was extremely nervous, not only as a teaching assistant, but even as a graduate student in the classroom. I had always struggled a bit with my self-confidence, but for the first time, I wanted to make myself invisible at school.

As a result, I quickly became depressed. I remember walking down the quiet streets of the suburbs and feeling helpless. I was not prepared to experience such a sudden and unexpected crisis. My mind told me to persevere, but my heart told me that the homesickness was unbearable. Then, within a month of my arrival, a tragedy that changed the course of world history occurred.

On the morning of Tuesday, September 11, 2001, I was in my suburban Chicago apartment. I had received a package and was trying to figure out who had sent it and if perhaps it was part of my orientation materials. Just before 10 a.m., Arzu called. "Have you heard the news?" she asked. I immediately thought of Türkiye and a possible earthquake, as if the world consisted only of my homeland. She urged me to turn on the TV, and I, like so many others, then saw the videos of planes hitting Manhattan skyscrapers, played over and over again. At first, I could not grasp the significance of the event. I did not even think of it as a terrorist attack, and I even thought that the American media was making a big deal out of an accident in the way they often hyped other stories. It sounds silly now, but at first, I was still distracted by the mysterious package. In just minutes though, I realized how serious the event was and wondered if it would be safe to take the subway to get to campus. Soon after, I received an email announcing that classes were canceled for the day.

I do not remember exactly how I spent the rest of September 11, but I do remember the shock and sadness on campus the next day. The professor I was assisting set aside the entire class time for students to express their feelings. I was surprised at the level of freedom of expression. One student said that he had always thought America was invincible, but now recognized that it was not true. A Black student said that her grandfather felt that the U.S. was being punished for what it had done to Blacks in America. It was remarkable and emotional in many ways.

The following weeks were especially hard for Muslims in the U.S. I had no difficulties personally, but many who were visibly Muslim, or even mistakenly identified as Muslim, suffered harsh reactions and were very concerned. I was walking down the street with my friend Arzu, who wears a headscarf, and a man in a passing car shouted to us, "Building bombs?" Initially, I did not even realize his comment was directed at us, but after he drove on, I realized it was because of my friend's headscarf. While suspicions and misunderstanding existed before the horrific attacks of September 11, since then, the Muslim faith has unfortunately been almost equated with terrorism for some in the U.S. and elsewhere.

I have always been prone to gloom and sadness, but the time I spent in Chicago was very painful. I berated myself. Studying in the U.S. was a dream come true; why did I feel so miserable? I was homesick to the bone and felt inadequate and hopeless. I felt very insecure at school because I was not a native English speaker, and it all became overwhelming.

I became more and more convinced that I was not ready to complete a doctorate in the U.S. By late October, I had come to the conclusion that I had to go back to Istanbul. My German crush Thomas talked to me on the phone for hours trying to dissuade me. He eventually became a bit annoyed and even stopped talking to me when I did not heed his advice.

If I could go back in time and change recent world events, I would prevent the attacks of September 11, 2001, which led to disaster for millions of people around the world. I would also change the course of events in my own life. I tend to believe that everything happens for a reason and that we learn from our experiences, but my first experience at graduate school in the U.S. was such a disappointment and felt like such a big mistake that I still want to undo that brief period.

In retrospect, I realize that my expectations of myself were excessive and that I reacted to circumstances emotionally. My English was proficient enough to be admitted to grad school, but I had naively thought I would be able to shine, as I was used to. Of course, being an immigrant is a challenge by definition. Looking back, I can see that I was hasty and did not give myself enough time to adapt to a new environment, but as usual, I was impatient.

On November 7, I was in Istanbul. I was relieved, but also felt like a failure. My mother was happy to see me back home. She had not really wanted me to go so far away alone. I wanted to do a master's in Istanbul, but I had missed the deadlines for that year; I had arrived in the middle of the semester. I suddenly had a lot of free time, but no idea what to do. I thought it would be a good time to learn a second foreign language and sign up for a gym. I started to learn German, which while practical, was probably influenced by my infatuation with Thomas, and I began to work out regularly at a gym that was popular at the time. In just a few months, I was more fit than I had ever been, but I was still sad and disappointed.

I spent most of my twenties searching for greater meaning in life. I thought religion would provide meaning, and it did, because belief in an eternal life after death motivated me to be a better person, but religion alone did not prevent me from feeling somewhat depressed almost constantly.

Thomas frequently returned to Istanbul, and we reconciled in late 2001. Given that I had a lot of free time and enduring affection for him, I saw him as often as possible. I enjoyed walks together around the city and helping him renovate his boat. Clinging to a platonic love undermined my already fragile self-confidence as a young woman, but I did not know any better. To him, I was not only a reliable friend in a foreign land, but I suspect it was also an ego boost. Nonetheless, he was generous and caring, and it was a valuable experience for me. Though I

**With Thomas,
Cannes Film Festival, May 2002**

felt first love later than many, it is an important rite of passage.

I had planned to apply to Boğaziçi University to continue my studies, but the graduate school did not offer a master's program that year. Not wanting to leave Istanbul, I applied for the master's program in international relations at Bilgi University. It was a relatively new school, but it had a liberal reputation that appealed to me.

The year 2001 also brought another decisive turn for Türkiye. Once again, society was shocked by a severe economic crisis. Political instability and poor economic stewardship led to panic and collapse. Foreign divestment eliminated a crucial source of state income and left the government with enormous budget deficits and an empty cupboard. An International Monetary Fund loan and privatization of some state-owned industries provided a measure of stabilization, but the public suffered greatly. Confidence in the government waned even further and income inequality grew.

When the Turkish lira was sharply devalued, millions of Turks became poorer overnight. I remember my father complaining about his business costs because he imported goods in U.S. dollars, but he always said that this was the only way his business could survive. Unemployment hit even educated, urban, white-collar workers. The strong family ties in Turkish society were critical to helping many of the unemployed weather the crisis.

The financial turmoil of 2001, the poor response to the earthquakes of 1999, and political instability led to widespread dissatisfaction. People were no longer satisfied with the establishment in Ankara. They desperately wanted new hope and new names. This desire for change gave politicians like Erdoğan a much-needed boost.

When the parliamentary elections were held in November 2002, all 550 seats in the Grand National Assembly were up for redistribution. Like most everyone else, I was fed up with the existing political parties and the status quo, but there was no party that represented my views. I thought that I would vote for the Liberal Democratic Party (LDP) to make a statement, even though it had no chance of entering parliament. My opinion then, as now, is that Türkiye is not yet ready for a truly liberal party. How liberal the LDP actually was is also a question, but the founder, Besim Tibuk, had often spoken to students while I was at Bilkent and had impressed me.

At the time, I had nothing against the political Islamist movement in Türkiye, though they had not yet won my vote. I was disturbed by the fact that the Kemalist state had repeatedly shut down Islamist parties and that this was so readily accepted. I was surprised that even students in a modern place like Bilkent University supported such political bans. It took courage for anyone to defend the Islamists' right to political participation, because you could easily be labeled one of them and suffer consequences. People in Türkiye have always found it difficult to distinguish between supporting a group's platform and supporting the group's right to exist. This disturbing intolerance is not unique to Türkiye, but it is clearly more prevalent in less democratic countries where polarization is established by the state.

One more in a long line, Erbakan's party, the RP, had been closed by the state in the 1990s. Another Islamically oriented political party, the Virtue Party (FP), was formed soon after, but it, too, was banned in 2001 for violating the secularist articles of the constitution. A reformist group within the party eventually split from the more traditional faction influenced by Erbakan and formed the Justice and Development Party (AKP) in August 2002.

The reformers believed that a strictly Islamist party would never be accepted and that a more moderate democratic conservative party that reflected Islamic values but without an Islamist agenda and one that expressed support for a liberal market economy and EU integration was a better option. The AKP or AK Party promised unsoiled politics and growth. "Ak" in Turkish means white, and the party took advantage of the fortunate acronym to assure the public that it represented a fresh, clean start and new solutions. They pledged to restore transparency and rebuild the devastated economy. They also appealed to those who resented that their faith and piety had been suppressed and maligned.

Abdullah Gül and Recep Tayyip Erdoğan were among the founders of the AKP. Though Erdoğan was the natural choice to lead the new party, given his oratory skill and success as mayor of Istanbul, he had been forced to leave that position in 1998. A court had found him guilty of inciting domestic unrest and religious hatred for, among other things, reciting a poem with religious imagery that was viewed as provocative. He served a brief prison sentence and was banned from politics.

On election day, November 3, 2002, when my father and I were on our way to the polling station, he asked me which party I intended to vote for. When I told him that I was planning to cast my ballot for the LDP, he said that it would be wasted since the party had no chance of getting past the 10 percent threshold required to gain seats in parliament. He added that Türkiye needed a one-party government and that it was time to support the AKP. I was not committed to any party, and after talking to my father about the potential for stability and development, I, too, voted for the AKP.

Many people must have had similar thoughts. The AKP won a landslide election victory and was given the opportunity to form a single-party government after a long period of failed coalitions. The only other party to win any seats was the CHP, but it and nine independents were clearly in the minority.

In my opinion, the AKP's victory was not unexpected, but apparently my fellow students in the Bilgi master's program were surprised. I have always been amazed at the inability or unwillingness of some members of the Turkish elite to recognize the realities of society. Some of my classmates despaired because they feared that Islamists had taken over the government and once again there were worries that Türkiye would slide into sharia law.

I disagreed. I believed that the AKP was sincere in its promise to lead Türkiye into the EU and that a more democratic and free country would benefit everyone. To me, it was a matter of enlightened national self-interest. However, the social pressure I felt at school after the election inhibited me from even thinking of expressing my opinion. Academics and elites who supported the AKP in the early years also experienced social pressure because of the Islamist label. Many, including members of the media and foreign observers, seemed pleased to see a modern, one-party government after long years of instability. There was significant support for the self-styled Muslim democrats, a reference to Christian democratic parties in Germany and elsewhere. "We have taken off our national [Islamist] shirt," Erdoğan declared, but some remained skeptical. While many in Türkiye and around the world hoped for a genuine, practical compromise, and initially that optimism appeared justified, it was not long before some of the suspicions would prove to be well founded.

The AKP initiated several modern and moderate policies, including some advanced by previous secular governments. Economic liberalization, privatization, measures to decentralize and democratize, and other areas that would aid EU candidacy were targeted for reform while maintaining an Islamic perspective. The goal of membership in the EU and the resulting changes to the political balance that decreased the influence of the military were widely popular.

Yet, despite the emphasis on Westernization from the earliest days of the republic, some Kemalists, particularly the military, were reluctant to relinquish their authoritarian control and adopt liberal democratic norms that would shield the Kurds, for example, as well as safeguard full participation of devout Muslims in the social, political, and economic spheres.

Notably, the burgeoning Muslim middle class saw EU membership as valuable in terms of economic opportunity and protection of their identity. However, some devout Muslims misinterpreted goals of modernity to mean economic freedom and consumerism without the need to internalize other correlating freedoms, rights, and responsibilities. It would sometimes evolve into a defense of their own lifestyle and right to be different while preventing others, such as the queer community as just one example, from enjoying the same rights. It also allowed for continued corruption and other offenses that undermine democracy.

In March of 2003, the new AKP government suffered a major defeat and unexpected crisis when the parliament did not approve allowing U.S. troops to use Türkiye as a base to launch an offensive as part of the 2003 invasion of Iraq. Public opinion in Türkiye was generally against the occupation of Iraq. Erdoğan had expressed desire to ally with the U.S. and he hoped to maintain good relations with European and other partners, but the initiative was soundly defeated when even a significant number of AKP members of parliament joined the opposition. The final vote was 264 votes in favor of the deployment, just short of the majority required by Turkish law. There were 250 "no" votes, 19 abstentions, and 17 absences. It was a shock to both the Turkish government and the U.S. government.

The AKP had pledged to restore the economy. They saw the refusal as threatening its progress and noted the obligation to protect its interests in a war that seemed inevitable. They cited the potential to have some influence in a postwar Iraq, a neighbor and former Ottoman territory. However, Turks are historically resistant to the idea of foreign troops on their soil, and a great many did not agree with the invasion and feared that the war would only damage the country's recovery. Many Turks also distrusted the promise of a $15 billion aid package, contending that much of the U.S. aid promised for help in the 1991 Persian Gulf War did not materialize.

I completed my coursework in the Bilgi master's program, but I had not given up on my dreams of going to the U.S. and began to think about a return. (I received my degree after submitting my thesis in 2006.) However, I was still nervous about going abroad alone and I decided to be more careful this time. I only applied to Temple University and to a master's program, rather than a Ph.D. program. A cousin was already studying there, and I thought that having someone in the family nearby would be helpful. I was very pleasantly surprised that not only was I accepted, but I was offered a scholarship as well. This was a needed lift to my confidence. I decided to accept Temple's offer.

By the summer of 2003, I was 24 years old and felt that I was up to the challenges of graduate school in America. I promised myself that I would not return without a degree.

CHAPTER 8

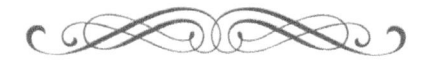

When I landed in Philadelphia in August 2003, the city did not initially seem very appealing, compared with the other places I had seen in the U.S. The Temple University campus is in a rough neighborhood. A professor in Türkiye who had earned her doctorate at Temple had told me of bullet holes in buildings and I saw that she had not exaggerated. It was not particularly scary, but it was not the dream campus I had seen in the movies, either. Nonetheless, though I was still self-conscious, especially as a foreigner, I liked Temple and felt that I would be able to persevere thanks to the warm and attentive faculty.

My cousin had arranged for me to stay temporarily with two Uzbek girls. I should have known that his standards might not meet my expectations. The girls were smart and hardworking, but they did not seem to care about their living environment. Not only was it a cheap old apartment, it was also a mess. It was one thing to temporarily sleep in a dirty apartment, but another to regularly see a mouse running along the baseboards.

Fortunately, I quickly found like-minded Turkish friends, such as Şeyma Aslan, who was studying engineering at nearby Drexel University. She was looking for a roommate and the timing could not have been better for me. She had already rented an apartment in University

City. When I mentioned the mice I had seen in my apartment, Şeyma surprised me by saying that it was not uncommon in Philadelphia. For the next two semesters, my biggest challenge was not graduate school, but the mouse problem I soon discovered in our apartment, too.

In my opinion, a house with mice was totally unacceptable and disgusting, but I was surprised at the reaction of my friends. They seemed to consider it almost normal. Since Şeyma did not want to move far from Drexel, I decided that I needed to find a mouse-free but still affordable apartment for myself.

In my second year, I moved into a studio in a highrise in Center City. Graduate school studies and teaching assistant responsibilities kept me busy, but I began to feel lonely. Graduate school can be isolating because you are always assigned more reading material and other assignments than you can handle, but being alone much of the time only made it more difficult. Luckily, I was in the city, and as someone who is from a metropolis like Istanbul, I felt alive there.

At my first baseball game, April 2004

Academically, the first two semesters were not easy, especially the courses on American politics, but I was willing to work hard. I was determined to succeed this time. Fortunately, I was assigned as a teaching assistant to a wonderful professor named Dr. Conrad Weiler. He even invited me to Thanksgiving dinner with his family during my first year. I have always appreciated his support, which has continued over many years.

I returned to Istanbul for the winter break. I was enjoying learning about a new culture and its society, but my life still very much revolved around Türkiye. I remember how shocked I was when, from thousands of miles away, I learned about four al-Qaeda suicide bombings in Istanbul in November 2003.

I now realize just how nationalistic Turks are raised to be, even the self-proclaimed liberals. Because of the time difference, I read all of the next day's Turkish newspapers online before going to bed. Of course, I met up with various classmates, especially in my second year, but my closest friends were still Turks. The Turkish diaspora has typically remained very centered on their Turkish identity rather than assimilating, no matter how much they benefit from their host country. There are exceptions, of course, and I believe this to be changing now, but it is still a truism to some extent.

By the end of my second year at Temple, I was doing well. I was offered another fellowship to continue in the Ph.D. program, but it was time for a change. I loved learning the theory of political science, but I was also eager to get out into the real world. Before traveling home for the summer break, I sent applications to several think tanks in Washington, D.C., with the hope of taking advantage of my one-year work permit.

In the summer of 2005, Türkiye was doing much better than it had during my youth. The economy was booming, the country had never come so close to the elusive goal of EU membership, and even non-Muslim minorities supported the Islamist-rooted AKP government because some rights had been restored and genuine progress was evident. In this climate, many Turks living abroad considered returning home.

Unfortunately, during that sunny period, my family was again shaken by something completely unexpected. My oldest sister, who was seven-and-a-half months pregnant, told us that her husband had left her. This was a complete shock, as it seemed to come without warning of any kind. He had seemed like a really decent guy. The next few months, if not years, were very stressful for all of us. I think that this shock and disappointment added to my distrust of men.

Temple University graduation, February 2006

Before I returned to Philadelphia in the fall, I received good news from Washington. The director of the Turkey Program at the Center for Strategic and International Studies (CSIS), Dr. Bülent Alirıza, had invited me for an interview. Needless to say, I was delighted.

During the exam period, due to my limited student budget, I stayed in an affordable but decent hotel called the Divine Lorraine Hotel in the West Philadelphia neighborhood of University City. It was run by an eccentric cult and had curious rules, such as requiring female guests to wear socks. It had been the first racially integrated hotel in the country, yet even in the 90s, had proscribed smoking, alcohol, cursing, and recommended modest dress and separation of men and women. Once again, I was amazed at the freedom of religion available in the U.S.

During that period before completing my degree, I happened to meet an American man who was interested in me. We were completely different and I knew it would not be a long-term relationship, but I welcomed the attention and affection. Eventually we parted ways, as expected, primarily because his life and his interests were rather limited. Like many, his life consisted almost exclusively of his immediate sphere of work and home, with only marginal interest or engagement in world events or broader issues.

In some ways, I feel that this is somewhat childlike, yet Americans have had the ability to be more withdrawn from world affairs because they have been prosperous, powerful, and less at the mercy of other nations. This sense of security, and often superiority, at least in some measure due simply to geography, can lead to a fundamental gap in understanding that has far-reaching implications, though international dynamics and interdependence have changed this to some degree in recent decades.

Having said that, of course, there are also many highly sophisticated individuals in the U.S. Some elite groups have historically led the rest of the country, despite claims of being a model of democracy, though that control has diminished in recent years and it could be said that the U.S. is seeing its own pendulum swing.

When I moved to Washington in the fall of 2005, my home country seemed to be moving forward like never before. Using an approach the government called "proactive diplomacy," Türkiye was opening up, not only to the West but also to the Middle East and Africa, in unprecedented ways. Erdoğan and his party had become something of a darling in the eyes of the international community as a poster child for a thriving Muslim democracy. But skeptics at home and abroad did not believe Erdoğan's expressed commitment to liberal principles. At the time, I never thought they would be proven correct. Along with many observers, I wanted to believe in the promise of modern political Islam.

I had been fortunate to secure an intern position at the prestigious CSIS by simply applying blindly, and as a young and enthusiastic aficionado of politics and international affairs, I was happy to have the opportunity to work there. Not knowing what my long-term job prospects might be, I arranged temporary accommodation with some Turkish students in Virginia. I enjoyed taking the metro to Farragut North station, not far from the

White House, and was excited to learn new things and meet new people. Alirıza was not an easy boss, but he was intelligent, respected, and had a great network, both in Washington and in Türkiye. I was able to meet and befriend intellectuals from Türkiye and elsewhere much more easily than I would have been at home.

There was an event in Washington almost every day for someone interested in politics and world events. Some days, you had a choice of several options. I was very eager to attend as many as I could. In addition to the small Turkish think tank community, representatives of the major Turkish media outlets also attended country-specific events. I was able to meet scholars such as Ömer Taşpınar, and journalists such as Ali Halit Aslan, Yasemin Çongar, Deniz Arslan, Ruşen Çakır, and Nuh Yılmaz—names that would later have great significance in Türkiye and in my own life.

Despite the overall positive image of Erdoğan and the AKP abroad, I saw the development of a suspicious campaign against the government in Washington in 2006. I attended almost every event related to Türkiye, and it was impossible not to feel the influence of neoconservatives. For example, former Pentagon official Michael Rubin and the once respectable but now noted Islamophobic conspiracist Frank Gaffney Jr. boldly claimed that Erdoğan and his party were turning Türkiye into an Islamofascist country.

My own experience later would give them at least some validation, but at the time, I did not see the signs. I thought the neoconservatives were exaggerating and ill-informed. I believed that at long last, Türkiye was definitively moving toward Europe in a way that also respected its Muslim heritage. At times in the early years, Erdoğan had tried to criminalize adultery and restrict abortion, for example, but he quickly backed down after public outrage. Any extreme impulses about lifestyle issues appeared to be contained. But to the die-hard secularists and neoconservatives, an Islamist was always an Islamist and was to be rejected.

As Alirıza has said, I have also often thought that the hatred of the AKP then was not because of what it did, but simply because of who it was. Despite all that we now know, I still think there is something to this in a world where there is a significant amount of Islamophobia. For instance, many people still consider the headscarf worn by the wives of AKP politicians to be a dangerous Islamist flag.

Having a similar religious background, I was convinced that it was just an expression of personal piety. I thought a lack of awareness, misunderstanding, and suspicion could be improved. However, I must admit that I missed some warning signs. I was so focused on the big picture that I thought most of Erdoğan's unacceptable remarks were inadvertent slips of the tongue, signs of ignorance, or otherwise pardonable mistakes and growing pains. I often took Erdoğan critics in Washington to task, even though I had no connection to or benefit from the government. I just did not think the detractors were being fair to an unusually successful government or giving it a chance.

To understand why so many ordinary Turks, even without a political Islamist agenda, supported Erdoğan and the AKP, it is important to understand the oppressive nature of the Kemalist ideology that ruled the country for decades with the help of the military-bureaucratic elite. The religious majority was deprived of their right to religious freedom for so long that they clung to whoever promised and delivered their long-violated rights. It is clear that the Kemalists' refusal to allow freedom of expression to anyone visibly devout and Erdoğan's manipulation of that grievance benefitted the AKP. Even after massive corruption allegations involving Erdoğan came to light in late 2013, a significant portion of society considers him better than the other options, including the CHP, which carries the legacy of oppressive secularism.

Many people dream of a dramatic, positive change, but in truth, it occurs only rarely and usually incrementally. In some ways, I had such a turning point in my life while in Washington. I may have received only a ridiculously small salary for my work at CSIS, but I met people who influenced the course of my life. One was veteran journalist Fehmi Koru, one of the first stars of the religious media in Türkiye. He was a good friend of Alirıza, and whenever Koru traveled to Washington, they would meet.

Alirıza once received an invitation from the Rumi Forum to attend an iftar dinner, a Ramadan fast-breaking meal, and he suggested that I go to the event in his place. I attended with Koru and Murat Yetkin, a secular journalist from the Doğan Media Group. The Rumi Forum is the representative NGO of the Gülen movement in Washington. In 2006, the movement was widely praised and on very good terms with the government of Türkiye. Many AKP representatives and others would visit Gülen while in the U.S. The iftar dinner was crowded, but Koru even introduced me to İbrahim Kalın, who served as President Erdoğan's spokesman and advisor, and is now director of the National Intelligence Organization. I happened to be seated with the first Muslim member of the U.S. Congress, Keith Ellison. When he asked a question about the headscarf debate, I explained that the issue has a particular significance in Türkiye. I could see that a religious scholar from the Gülen movement, Ahmet Kurucan, was listening intently to my remarks. He probably did not expect a pro-headscarf freedom stance from a Turkish woman who did not cover her hair. Koru, too, must have taken note and been sufficiently pleased by my defense of religious freedom that he posted a link to one of my blog posts in his widely read column after his return to Türkiye. I only realized where a spike in the traffic on my personal blog had originated when my friends called and told me of the link. Koru soon became something of a mentor to me.

I also recall that while I was living in Washington, a Turkey expert said that Professor Ahmet Davutoğlu, who served as an advisor to Erdoğan before becoming foreign minister and then prime minister, was "more dangerous" because of his sincere belief in political Islamism and a neo-Ottoman vision. I took this comment with a grain of salt, given my belief that comments about AKP members tended to be influenced by prejudice.

At the time, there was no obvious indication that the seemingly mild-mannered and moderate academic Davutoğlu would prove to be as autocratic as he was, especially once he was chosen by Erdoğan as his successor in 2014. The U.S. description of Davutoğlu as an "exceptionally dangerous" Islamist influence dating back to 2004 and published by Wikileaks in 2010 should also have set alarm bells ringing, but he was largely perceived as weak and a placeholder.

In my defense, I had reason to be skeptical of the assumptions of different camps, both internal and external. Türkiye has always been a polarized country, especially—though not exclusively—along the fault line of the role of secular and religious identity and freedom. Personally, I believe it is possible to defend a liberal version of secularism and be a devout Muslim at the same time, but the prevailing atmosphere and mindset has generally forced one to choose sides.

For a while, the AKP convinced not only people like me, but also the EU, the U.S. government, and international media, that it could realize the successful combination of religiosity and secularism, overcoming the cultural conflict of what the controversial author Samuel Huntington called a "torn country." However, it turned out to be a marriage of convenience tolerated by the AKP until Islamists consolidated power.

At that point in the early 2000s, it was still too early for those who wanted to believe that change had finally come to credit the claims of red flags regarding the AKP and Erdoğan, especially given alarming signals of the continued activity of the deep state.

When a gunman opened fire in a Turkish courthouse on May 17, 2006, killing a judge and wounding four others, the deputy head of the Council of State, Tansel Çölaşan, claimed that the assailant had shouted, "I am the soldier of God" and "Allah is the most great" (Allah-u akbar), and that the act was in response to a court ruling against teachers wearing Muslim headscarves. The next day, the most influential newspaper in Türkiye, *Hürriyet*, called the incident "Turkey's September 11" and there was significant outrage before any evidence corroborating a religious motive was found. I was in Washington when I read that headline, and I was angry. I thought that some forces were trying to interfere in civilian politics because the AKP had been successful.

The phrase "Allah-u akbar" is misunderstood, much like "jihad" and other Arabic words or concepts such as sharia law, and it has sadly become another dog whistle to provoke fear and thoughts of terrorism. In reality, it is an ordinary expression used in a variety of contexts to recognize the power and grace of God.

Subsequent investigation of the courthouse shooting revealed that the perpetrator was not religious at all. There were allegations that he and family members had received payment for the attack, and that it may have been orchestrated by a retired gendarmerie general who was later detained in another case on conspiracy charges.

The judge also subsequently admitted that she did not, in fact, hear the shouts she had reported and retracted her statement. It is my belief that this event was designed to foment upheaval in the run-up to the 2007 presidential election. Çölaşan, also president of the Atatürkist Thought Association, would also later be officially reprimanded and face legal action for criticism of the results of the 2010 referendum, saying that those who had voted in favor of constitutional amendments were uneducated, whereas the "no" voters were the educated group of society.

Ultimately, it was decided that her comments fell within her right to freedom of expression.

Seda Çiftçi, a long-time staffer of the CSIS Turkey Project, became a good friend. She was warm, kind, and sensitive. I often wondered why she worked in politics rather than teaching kindergarten, for example. In mid-2006, Seda was going to move to a position at another institution and Alirıza promised me a full-time position. I was relieved to have a plan in place and did not look further for another job. However, when Seda ultimately had to stay at CSIS, I realized that I should have had a Plan B and not considered an offer that was not in writing to be a certainty.

I loved being in the nation's capital, but Washington is expensive. After my temporary stay with Turkish girls close to the Gülen movement, I wanted more privacy. A Korean-American student who was living alone in her parents' house in nearby Vienna, Virginia was looking for a roommate, and I decided to give it a try. This was also my introduction to Korean culture, which in some ways, was similar to my own. For example, like Turks, Koreans do not wear outdoor shoes in the house. Our arrangement was quite comfortable, and I stayed there until I had to leave CSIS in November 2006 because my work permit had expired. Since I did not have another job that would permit me to stay, I had no choice but to go home.

CHAPTER 9

Social tension in Türkiye increased as the presidential election approached. Since the parliament elected the president, it was very likely that someone from the AKP would take over in 2007 and concern about a perceived threat of Islamic fundamentalism taking hold of daily life surged once again. Large rallies were held to support the idea of a strictly secular government.

Beginning in April 2007, what are known as the Republic Protests drew enormous crowds in several cities and garnered international attention. Just days after the first protest, then-Prime Minister Erdoğan announced that the AKP candidate would be the serving foreign minister, Abdullah Gül, rejecting proposals by the opposition CHP to nominate a non-partisan, mutually acceptable figure. The presidency was primarily a symbolic position at the time, and some thought that Erdoğan preferred to retain a seat with more power.

The Gül candidacy meant that a man whose wife wears the religious headscarf could ascend to the nation's highest office and reside in Çankaya Palace in Ankara. For many, this prospect was intolerable. Since the founding of the republic, the official presidential office and residence had been a secularist bastion. Atatürk had purchased the large property, and it has great symbolic value. For the other half of the nation, however, it was time for the pious to be recognized by the state.

Erdoğan has many times said that conservatives and Islamists were the "Blacks" of Türkiye, using racist rhetoric to emphasize his appeal to the "average" Turk in contrast to snobby elites; he was just a simple man trying to get things done for the nation. "They think we don't know anything about art and music. They think we are negroes," he said in 2013.

Erdoğan had long relied on placing himself among those who were not of the upper class, those who faced discrimination, and the trope of "black Turks" and "white Turks" as divisive language that was largely classist with undertones of racism was well worn by 2013, though the term used in Turkish is a bit more ambiguous than in English. In addition to reflecting a generally abhorrent strategy of divide and conquer, though ever useful around the globe, there is in fact a very small population of Black Turks who are descendants of emancipated African slaves who were brought to Anatolia and they, along with other segments of the population, have faced broad discrimination.

Nonetheless, Erdoğan capitalized on racism to polarize, as he has used antisemitism and other points of division. This is the same man who also said, "Unity, togetherness, solidarity; these are the things we need most. We can overcome many problems so long as we treat each other with love," in 2007.

While ostensibly organized by NGOs, notably headed by the Atatürk Thought Association, and opposition politicians, *Nokta* magazine published documents in 2007 indicating that some of the organizers of the protest rallies were linked to the military, which cast a shadow on the civilian nature of the protests. The protests were clearly meant as a warning to the AKP.

I took sides in this conflict without hesitation. Along with many others, I was frustrated by the methods of the establishment and what I thought were excessive fears of a non-secular orientation. I thought it was a shame that the religious headscarf was seen as an unacceptable obstacle and could not be respected as a personal choice.

Opponents used parliamentary procedure to block the proceedings. A boycott led to the lack of a quorum of 367 parliamentarians to provide the necessary two-thirds majority and the failure of Gül's candidacy in the first and second rounds, despite securing a majority of the votes cast.

A former judge, Sabih Kanadoğlu, argued that the majority required by the constitution to elect the president had not been met, which led to a crisis. The same day, April 27, 2007, the Turkish Armed Forces released a statement warning that they would not hesitate to become involved as guardians of secularism. Called an "e-memorandum" veto coup because the visible military activity was limited to a memorandum posted on the official Turkish Armed Forces website, it nonetheless increased tension between the AKP and the military.

Chief of General Staff Yaşar Büyükanıt called for the new president to be a true secularist, and in subsequent rallies, chants included slogans such as "We are the soldiers of Mustafa Kemal." Everyone was angry. I became so frustrated with public attitudes, efforts to undermine the legitimacy of the elected government, and the military's intervention that I joined a political protest in the streets for the first time.

A newly formed youth organization called Young Civilians (Genç Siviller) organized protest events to express disapproval of military involvement in affairs of state and discrimination of any kind. They became successful in part due to their creative use of humor and satire. After the e-memorandum, I accepted their email invitation to protest against the military in the heart of Istanbul in Taksim Square. I joined a group of young people I did not know to "search" for justice one evening with flashlights and I remember speaking to some foreign media correspondents that night in English. It seemed that it was the least I could do to counter the establishment and express my opinions.

Unfortunately, the Young Civilians were apparently later co-opted by the AKP government, diminishing my faith in the longevity of independent movements in Türkiye. Visible members of this group turned into pro-government columnists and activists. It was revealed in 2015 that they were paid by a lobbying firm hired by the AKP to improve the government's image, especially abroad.

After considerable additional unrest and wrangling, including proposed changes to the procedure for the presidential election, in a deft political move, Erdoğan called for early elections, saying that he wanted the public to have a say in the presidential election. A snap election was held in July 2007 to resolve the deadlock and the AKP gained an even larger proportion of the vote.

Gül was finally elected in the third round of a second attempt to elect the president in August when the nationalist MHP resolved to be present in parliament to settle the quorum issue. The crisis had already reached such a level that the matter had been brought to the Constitutional Court and amendments to the constitution were proposed. These included allowing the public to elect the president, rather than the parliament; provisions to hold general elections every four years, rather than five; and to reduce the length of the presidential term of office.

Meanwhile, I was trying to figure out what to do with my life and I was discouraged by the prospects at home. It was important to me to participate in the election, but after thinking about my options, I did not think I would be happy remaining in Istanbul. I had often been homesick in the U.S., but it seemed to offer better opportunity, so I applied to rejoin the Ph.D. program at Temple University. I was admitted and began preparing to return to Philadelphia.

In August 2007, I was back in the U.S. Temple was a familiar and friendly place, but knowing the housing problems in Philadelphia and realizing that my cohort had moved on, I decided to try living in the suburbs. A couple of college friends lived in North Wales, and I thought that I would have some company if I rented an apartment in the same complex. That did not work out the way I expected.

I commuted to Temple a few days a week in an old Nissan Sentra that I had bought from a friend, but with a new group of classmates, Temple did not feel the same and I was secluded living in the suburbs. Maybe it was a lack of motivation, maybe my Ph.D. program felt boring after the lively environment in Washington, but despite my efforts and resolve, I quickly fell into the trap of isolation and depression.

That fall, I attended an event featuring an address Erdoğan gave to Turks living in the New York City area. I even asked him a question about the expansion of freedoms in Türkiye: "When will Turkey become a country that understands that diversity is wealth?" While considering his response, he correctly guessed which province of Türkiye my family originally came from based on my last name, and this anecdote even made it into some newspapers the next day. He appeared to appreciate the question, and doubtless it served him well to have the opportunity to profess a desire for unity when appearing before an international audience.

Today, I know more about his true attitudes, but at that time, Erdoğan seemed to be in favor of relaxing all kinds of bans in Türkiye, and I was still very frustrated about discrimination based on identity. My sincere belief in the value of diversity has not changed. Erdoğan had always been unapologetically conservative; however, he hid his true opinions and agenda under the guise of seemingly wanting Türkiye to become more like a country of Western Europe. The public appeal of this goal served his own interests, as we would all soon learn.

In October 2007, a referendum was held in which the public approved Erdoğan's proposal to elect the president by popular vote and make other changes to the constitution. The balance of power had been altered and the influence of the military had been weakened. The night of the landslide victory against the establishment, my father hung a huge Turkish flag outside our apartment building. This was his response to the neighbors who had flocked to the rallies to prevent the election of an AKP president. However, in the new hybrid system, power struggles between the president and the government would be inevitable unless there was strong one-man rule. Had the secularists been reasonable and liberal on the headscarf issue, Türkiye could perhaps have spared itself prolonged years of Erdoğan at the helm and the abuse of religion in politics.

One day, I was at a friend's house near New York City. I casually decided to check on my friend and first love, Thomas. I had not heard from him in some time. My painful love for him was long gone, but we had remained good friends. He had been working in the United Arab Emirates and pursuing his crazy dreams, as usual. A few years earlier, he had traveled to Antarctica, and I had not been at all surprised when he had said he wanted to climb Mount Everest. I had occasionally followed his Everest adventure through a website he told me about and wanted to catch up with his stories. When I read that Thomas had died during the descent, I could not believe my eyes. In disbelief, I asked my friend to read me the relevant passage. She confirmed the terrible news. I did not cry right away, probably because it seemed unreal, but the loss of the connection we shared was profound. He was one of the most amazing people I had ever met and a significant part of my life story.

By the late fall of 2007, I was truly depressed in my Philadelphia suburb. More and more, I realized that a Ph.D. was not the right path for me. Academia felt one-dimensional and remote. But how could I quit and go home again after trying so hard to come back? I wrestled with what to do and was worried about what other people would think, but I did not want to go crazy in solitude just to get a Ph.D. that I didn't even want.

While I had always liked the structure in the U.S. and living in a liberal democratic society, I was also used to being part of a big family and enjoying a very active social life. Soon after some friends from the Gülen movement learned about my plans to return home, the head of the Rumi Forum asked me to work for them in Washington. There was no concrete job offer, and I knew it would be as poorly paid as a teaching assistant with even more work; however, my first reason for turning down the job was that I would still be alone. I thought I would rather be with my family and live a normal life than suffer in solitude in the U.S., even while among friends from the movement. Yet it was only after a trip to Mecca that I was able to regain my courage and sense of direction.

During the 2007 semester break, my parents and one of my sisters were scheduled to make the pilgrimage to Mecca. All Muslims who can afford it are obliged to perform this sacred journey, the hajj, at least once in their lifetime. As I was very unhappy and uncertain about my life and future, I asked God to help me find my way out of my troubles. At close to the last minute, I insisted that I wanted to join my family on their trip. I hurriedly filled out all of the required paperwork and sent my passport to Istanbul to apply for a visa to enter Saudi Arabia. There was a risk of not getting my passport back before my flight from Philadelphia to Istanbul and the wait was very stressful, but fortunately, it was returned in time.

Once I arrived in Istanbul, I joined my family as they set out on the journey. Our pilgrimage was shorter than some, but long enough to meet the requirements. It was nonetheless very intense, both emotionally and physically. I told only very close friends, not just because of the stigmatization of Muslim observance in Türkiye, but also because I wanted to keep it private. The experience was a special opportunity and helped me to evaluate my life and figure out what I wanted. I was very glad that I had made the decision to participate.

When I got back to Philadelphia, I was certain that I did not want to spend yet more years of my life alone in a Ph.D. program. It was hard to tell the department that I would be leaving when they had accepted me a second time, but I had to do what I believed was best for me. I felt relief after I dropped out of the program, despite some concern about prying questions and an unknown future. I was confident that it was the right decision. It was not just the isolation I experienced being far from home, but also the isolation of academia. Maybe I should have tried to integrate more, but at that time it was simply not the right environment for me. The U.S. chapter of my life was over, or so I thought. I had no idea what fate had in store for me.

CHAPTER 10

In February 2008, I was back home again and determined to build a new life with the valuable experience I had gained in the U.S. When I told Fehmi Koru, the prominent journalist I had met in Washington, that I was back for good and looking for a job, he said he could refer me to his best friend, a Mr. Gül, who happened to be the new president. Koru said that the president could use someone with my skills on his internal team. I have to say that it was exciting to hear that. It would be a dream come true to work near the president.

A short time later, Koru told me that when he had spoken to the president about me, First Lady Hayrünnisa Gül had expressed interest and wanted me to join her team. As a naive newcomer to the world of the professional bureaucracy, I assumed that I would easily be able to demonstrate the necessary talent to soon move from the first lady's staff into a more political position that would better suit my interests.

Before long, a close aide to the new president, Ayşe Yılmaz, invited me to the presidential residence for an interview. I was thrilled. Instead of asking for transportation, I decided to drive to Ankara with my father. It may sound somewhat unusual or even unprofessional, but he was also eager to share the experience and it's quite normal in Türkiye for a father to accompany his daughter, no matter how old she may be.

I had a preliminary interview at Çankaya Palace with the first lady and Yılmaz in March 2008. While we were waiting for First Lady Gül, I found out that Yılmaz, who was six years older than I, had also attended Bilkent University. We happened to have mutual friends who belonged to the Gülen movement. I knew that the AKP and the religious movements crossed paths, but I was still a bit surprised because political Islamists would ordinarily tend to maintain some distance from the non-political and non-Islamist Gülen movement. She had worked for Gül in the party, but when he was appointed foreign minister, she switched to working in the residence because of the headscarf ban. She was a close family confidant who was out of the limelight.

With First Lady Gül, Çankaya Palace, March 2008

My initial impression of First Lady Gül could not have been better. We had a good conversation and I answered all of her questions enthusiastically, probably in more detail than necessary. She seemed impressed with me and I was hopeful. I knew that she had experienced discrimination because of her use of the headscarf, not only during the presidential election, but also when she had not been able to enroll at Ankara University some years prior due to the ban in place, despite having passed the entrance exams. I was eager to help the new presidential couple reshape the status quo.

A few days later, I was notified by the president's office that I was to have a second interview with Nursuna Memecan, a businesswoman and an AKP deputy from Istanbul. I was surprised, as she had no official connection to the president's office. Our conversation in her Taksim apartment was tense. I think that perhaps in her eyes I was not sufficiently deferential. When she suggested that I was indecisive, based on my resume, I responded that not everyone is born with the same comfortable opportunities she had. Apparently, our dislike was mutual, and our subsequent relationship was always strained.

It was only later that I fully realized how closely connected she was to the Gül family. Memecan came from an elite family. This contributed to her appeal for Mrs. Gül, who was from a much more modest background and I think wanted very much to be accepted and approved of. Frankly, I suspect that the attention Memecan paid to the Gül family was not sincere. She was not the only one to ingratiate themself with the powerful, but I was appalled at how blind the powerful were to insincere praise and sycophancy.

Despite my uncomfortable conversation with Memecan, the first lady must have liked me and I was hired. On April 14, 2008, I started a probationary employment period of a rather ill-defined job at Çankaya

Palace. When I walked through Gate 5 of the palace on the first day, I was full of excitement and enthusiasm. I truly believed that I could be part of a positive change.

Çankaya Palace is, in fact, hardly palatial and was a great disappointment. The office space was no different from an average, outdated, depressing government building. It was nice to be in a large compound in the middle of the forest, a rarity in the country's capital, but aside from that, you could all but smell the bureaucracy in the air.

The original residence, dating to at least the early 1900s, had been expanded and modernized to some extent over the years, but the complex of buildings was still modest and showing its age. Once he became president, Erdoğan built an extravagant and controversial new presidential palace complex, with at least 1,100 rooms and an official price tag of at least $615 million.

I began to look for what I could do to assist in the first lady's office. On April 17, I was briefly introduced to the president when he visited the offices. I was surprised that he paid attention to the decorations and the cleanliness of the carpets. I had assumed that people in high office were too concerned with important policy issues to pause for such details.

A few weeks later, I was called to the presidential residence. The Güls had remained in the official residence of the minister of foreign affairs because the historic "Pink House," the home of Turkish presidents since 1932, was in poor condition. I soon spent less and less time in the presidential office and more in the residence. It was a great privilege to have this degree of access and work so close to the president's family. However, my views on this experience would change significantly over time.

At one point during my first few months of work at Çankaya, I received a call from the president's chief of staff, also the former head of the president's private secretariat and an ambassador, Hüseyin Avni Karslıoğlu. He said that the president was impressed with my comments in a column I had written for an English-language daily newspaper, *Today's Zaman*.

Naturally, I was pleased with the praise. A few days later, as I was leaving the presidential residence late in the evening, the first lady asked me to go upstairs to the living room. It would be my first truly personal encounter with the president. "Is it really you who writes these opinion pieces?" was the first thing he asked. I can now see the potential problems associated with this activity, but the line of appropriate interaction between media and politics in Türkiye is somewhat blurred.

President Gül in a previously unpublished photo, the presidential residence, 2010

The president also asked me about my background, how I had learned English so well, my family, and so on. He was very gracious and welcoming. Although I was working in the first lady's office, President Gül encouraged me to attend as many briefings as possible and to continue to follow political matters and share my insights with him. I thought it was an opportune time to indicate my desire to join the president's team because the first lady was also present and heard his remarks, but I did not yet know how great her influence was over her husband. Though she focused on the traditional concerns of a first lady, she was also very involved in daily decisions and affairs beyond that scope. She was, in a way, the unofficial chief of staff. I did not know that I was, as one co-worker put it some years later, working for the first de facto female president of the country.

My probationary period lasted for about two months and then I was officially appointed to the palace on June 9, 2008. I had not aspired to a career in public service and so it meant little to me beyond the obvious honor, but it was of great importance to everyone else. After all, a civil service post meant job security, and this was a position of some prestige.

I was a young devout Muslim, but also familiar with the Western world, which was still a somewhat rare combination in my generation. I knew that my credentials and experience were valuable, but when I occasionally spoke English with colleagues, this apparently threatened and irritated some of the loyalists who did not have the same qualifications.

With my parents at a wedding, Istanbul, 2009

Ambassador Karslıoğlu spoke to me in English whenever he saw me after reading my commentary in *Today's Zaman*. When he encouraged me to take the exam to become a professional diplomat before I turned 30, which was the maximum age for beginning a career in the diplomatic service, I did not see why I should give up an interesting job in the nation's highest office. I was young, idealistic, and ambitious; I just did not know what I did not know.

The first six months at Çankaya were exciting. I was happy to see, meet, and talk with numerous prominent individuals. Not long after I started, Türkiye hosted very important guests at the presidential palace, including the then-monarch of the British Commonwealth, Queen Elizabeth II, and Prince Philip. First Lady Gül put a lot of effort into this visit, wanting to ensure that it was suitably grand and well executed.

I remember that she ordered a custom-made, tulip-shaped brooch for the queen from an Armenian jeweler in Istanbul. While many may associate tulips with the

Netherlands, they originate in Central Asia and were first cultivated by Turks. They became a symbol of power and beauty in the Ottoman Empire and continue to be a widely used motif today. I also recall the queen's unique style, including a distinctive evening gown with a pattern of grape clusters.

I thought that this environment was a great beginning, and it lifted my spirits and hopes for my career. One day, a semi-academic journal called *Insight Turkey*, published by the Foundation for Political, Economic, and Social Research (SETA), a pro-government think tank, contacted me and asked for an article. I liked being taken seriously and without giving much thought to the independence of the publication, wrote an article about how the pending case for the closure of the ruling AKP based on the principle of separation of religion and state would be a blow to democracy. The case ultimately failed by one vote.

With President Gül, summer 2010
(Photo courtesy of presidential photographer)

In retrospect, however, I must admit that I was naive and idealistic. The president appreciated my capabilities from the start and asked me to do things like prepare the English version of his biography and content for the president's official website, but perhaps for a related reason, the first lady's attitude toward me quickly degenerated. In the summer of 2008, she said that she wanted me to continue to work for her to protect me from possible bullying on President Gül's team. At the time, I believed she had my interests in mind.

I could feel that some inner circle employees were not happy about a dynamic young employee joining the team. My lack of experience in "real life" or office politics did not help. I was a complete novice and had no idea of the level of the games played behind closed doors. When I realized the extent of the truly Byzantine plots inside Çankaya, I mentioned it to my mentor Koru. He said that the president's team was likely intimidated by me and trying to block me. He was right, but even he missed the biggest piece of the puzzle: It was the first lady herself who wanted to control me to satisfy her own ego and maintain influence. I resisted this thought until my last months at the palace, but I came to believe that it was Mrs. Gül who did not want me to move forward in my career and others followed her lead.

Even at the highest levels, a culture of fear was pervasive. With few exceptions, public officials tended to bully their subordinates while ingratiating themselves with their superiors. It was power that was respected, rather than the individual, which only increased the intimidation and egos of those with authority. I was unprepared and unwilling to play this game. It was a rude and disappointing awakening.

The Turkish bureaucracy is highly politicized, and loyalists are appointed to senior positions. While it is difficult to remove civil servants, they can be marginalized, and so, many choose to ingratiate themselves and curry favor rather than face a transfer or leave their position. There is little in the way of a merit-based system, and outsiders are not easily accepted for fear that they will conspire against those in power.

CHAPTER 11

Events of 2007 and 2008 marked a turning point for the nation. Specifically, the now infamous and immensely important Ergenekon investigations and trials. Türkiye has long been fertile ground for conspiracy theories, real and imagined, and that remains true today. Many believe that a shadowy deep state organization interferes in, if not controls, the government, and that foreign powers also intervene with nefarious designs. The revelations of clandestine ties and activities exposed by the Susurluk incident and others confirmed some truth to the notion of the deep state but were also fodder for broad speculation and manipulation.

Ergenekon, the name of a valley in a Turkic salvation myth, became synonymous with a secular, ultra-nationalist criminal organization allegedly determined to control the government. The strong mandate and success of the AKP since the 2007 election had humbled the previously very politically powerful military. This did not sit well with many. While there was no doubt some truth to the initial discoveries of activities attributed to the group, it would become another example of abuse of power.

A series of shocking events that to this day remain somewhat murky set the stage for investigations and trials that would go on for years and have a fateful impact on the country. There had been whispers and reports of a deep state Ergenekon group before, but the claims of a minor criminal who had been arrested in 2001 purporting to have knowledge of this secret network dedicated to plots designed to protect the secular establishment were the impetus for the furor to come.

The Ergenekon investigation, launched in 2007 following the recovery of a stash of illegal arms, was framed as a move to clean house and eliminate subversive elements accused of all manner of destabilization, including the use of false flag operations.

These efforts allegedly included the courthouse shooting in 2006; the bombing of the shop of a former member of the PKK; the assassination of the Turkish-Armenian human rights journalist Hrant Dink, who promoted recognition of the Armenian genocide and reconciliation, but had been prosecuted for denigrating the republic and received numerous death threats from Turkish nationalists; the publication by the political news magazine *Nokta* of purported military plans to stage a takeover of the AKP government; separate murders of a Catholic priest and a bishop, as well as three Christians, a German national, and two Turkish converts who published Christian Bibles; among other disturbing incidents. The discoveries of significant caches of weapons and documents thrust the story into the spotlight.

Prosecutors alleged that Ergenekon was a vast organization committed to destabilizing and overthrowing the AKP government. They claimed that the group was responsible for terrorist attacks and involved in extortion and drug trafficking, as well as virtually every act of violence in the previous decades, from those previously attributed to the PKK to violent Islamists. They asserted that they had found evidence of various coup plots and other classic deep state operations. Arrests of numerous military and police officers, journalists, academics, and others followed.

Various events were collocated into the indictments and harsh sentences were imposed, despite inconsistencies and questionable evidence (some later confirmed to be falsified) in some cases. Fethullah Gülen, though living abroad, also faced new accusations of participation in the manipulation of the prosecutions and a desire to eventually establish an Islamic state.

The entire narrative was hyped relentlessly, and defensiveness and paranoia on all sides increased. All parties had some reasonable grounds for fear, anger, and a sense of injustice, but the result was even greater polarization and continued confusion and conspiracy claims.

There were some worries that a group within the military had or could become frustrated and take matters into their own hands, and some evidence supports this anxiety. However, notably, claims against AKP supporters or some alleged deep state activities were excused or not pursued, and there was pressure and punishment meted out for any who questioned the integrity of the proceedings. For example, the Doğan Media Group suddenly faced enormous and extended tax investigations and fines for critical coverage of the government. This technique had been used in the past and continues to be a disgraceful tool used by the state.

The investigation was initially lauded by many both at home and abroad as a step toward further democratization, transparency, and accountability. But it would become a wide-ranging and extremely controversial source of conflict. To the secularists, it was a politically motivated effort to discredit those who opposed the AKP. Kurds and other groups welcomed examination of the deep state, but also viewed the proceedings with some suspicion.

The truth would now seem to be that all parties were affected by some degree of mis- or disinformation, defensiveness, and manipulation of some valid concerns. While some political motivation for the scrutiny seems to be apparent, it is also fair to say that many were at least initially sincere in their belief that it was critical to bring the military and others to heel. Projective reasoning and loyalty likely contributed to the immensely complicated events that would occur, including a more authoritarian state rather than the promised pluralistic democracy.

It is not much in doubt that there was indeed a Gladio-type organization established in Türkiye in the 1950s; however, just how it morphed over time and what its structure and activities were is less clear. All sides have used the notion of a powerful clandestine organization to suit their objectives. It is most likely that Ergenekon was never the monolithic organization it has been purported to be, but rather that there were several cells that operated with a large degree of impunity and independence to preserve the "proper" (secular nationalist) character of the state, at times by any means deemed necessary. Just how individual groups may have been corrupted, just what they did, or just how much the entire notion was manipulated may never be known.

SEVGİ AKARÇEŞME

During the height of the initial Ergenekon investigations, I worked in the country's top office, but I have to say that I was so preoccupied with the internal crises and survival within Çankaya Palace that I simply accepted what Deputy Prime Minister Arinç and others said about it being a matter of cleansing the state apparatus. After all, some deep state activities and motivations had already seemingly been made clear.

The liberal daily *Taraf* published numerous apparently incriminating documents and audio recordings were released of a general, Çetin Doğan, who spoke about a coup attempt project codenamed "Sledgehammer" (Balyoz), and he did not repudiate the alleged plan. In retrospect, I wish I had paid more attention to the claims of falsified evidence and more, but the theory that there was a sophisticated network plotting against the government and the Gülen movement was plausible.

Though now much has been thrown into doubt and certainty of details is all but impossible, I nonetheless still think that the exposure of forces that intended to subvert democracy is valuable. Though courts and others later concluded that the Ergenekon network may not ever have even existed, we know that official judgments can be manipulated, and I cannot understand complete rejection of the concept.

The defendants and others accused the Gülen movement of orchestrating and unduly promoting the trials, using the tried-and-true formula for division, even though Erdoğan himself was in charge and even publicly took over the cases, saying that he was the prosecutor. Anyone who knows Türkiye knows that such a critical investigation would not have been conducted without the government's approval or encouragement. However, the press did play a role in public understanding of the matter, including media associated with the Gülen movement. I think that there was genuine belief in hidden efforts to foment chaos, but I firmly believe that if anyone close to the Gülen movement followed unlawful or improper orders from Erdoğan or anyone else, they should be held personally accountable.

I distinctly remember First Lady Gül's support for the investigations. In private conversations, she said that she and her husband knew about military plots to undermine the government. Yet, though she was in the midst of all the turmoil in Türkiye, I do not think she was fully aware of or appreciated the serious consequences that military intervention would have. She was primarily obsessed with getting things organized in the residence. One day we were in one of the large storage rooms and as she gazed at all their belongings, she lamented, "How are we going to be able to transport all these things in the event of a coup?" I am still amazed at her priorities.

There was an unusual division of labor in the palace. The president's opportunistic head of security, Osman Çangal, a former police chief, was also something of a de facto head of the cabinet. He was not qualified for such a position, and to secure his status, he knew he had to demonstrate loyalty and please the first lady before anyone else. Virtually the entire staff showed him a false respect. When I refused to call him "boss" like other new hires, he excluded me from his protection. I was too proud to show him undeserved deference and we always had a dysfunctional relationship.

One day, I found a harassing message at my door. This was strange because my apartment was on the presidential property; no random outsider could get through the checkpoints. When I told Çangal about it, he asked me not to mention anything to the first lady and to bring the note to him. His investigation turned up nothing. Call me paranoid, but I even suspected that the message might have been an attempt by him or the first lady herself to intimidate me.

The first lady made a big fuss when I wanted to move from my basement apartment to a better one, and her team followed suit. In my opinion, such matters are too insignificant to be handled by the first family, but First Lady Gül took every opportunity to exert control and denigrate me in the eyes of everyone in Çankaya, including the president.

I enjoyed having such a privileged job and had hoped to be a part of making positive change in the country, but the unpleasantness of the conditions only increased. Though domineering and belittling behavior is not unusual to some degree for staffers to high-profile individuals, it was not the role I envisioned for myself, and I found it hard to accept. There were many times that I considered leaving this job that had been so promising because I was disappointed and disillusioned. I was able to enjoy a fancy office in the beautiful hills of Istanbul at the summer palace and other perks, but like all of the other staff, from ambassadors to the household staff, I was always nervous. No one ever knew what might anger the first lady and prompt a fit of rage. Not even the president was immune to her angry outbursts.

I realized that things in the first lady's realm were not what I had anticipated. I had been naive, but my eyes were soon opened to reality. For example, she frequently said to others that I was not ready to accompany her on foreign visits though there was no one in the first lady's office who spoke better English, and I had always expressed a willingness and the ability to be helpful. Instead, she brought her press secretary, who did not know a single word of any foreign language.

It was apparent to everyone that the first lady was deliberately preventing me from any opportunity to excel, but I persevered. I often made the joke that I was the Cinderella of the presidential palace, doing thankless work while everyone else went out partying, but alas, I had no prince in sight. Though I can honestly say that given the often unnecessary expense of these taxpayer-funded official trips and other behavior I cannot condone, I am glad today that I was not there for all but a few.

First Lady Gül was an extremely demanding and difficult boss, but her tenacity in overcoming various taboos in protocol and respect deserves recognition. In the early years of her tenure, she was not allowed to walk the red carpet with the president when receiving foreign counterparts because the headscarf was still stigmatized. Instead, she received visiting first ladies at another gate where there were no members of the press. She was also prevented from passing through the top general's residential area adjacent to the palace. She understandably viewed these practices as a personal insult and thought that if she could prove to the secular establishment that she was at least as smart, hardworking, and stylish as they were, they would see the person beneath the headscarf.

She had many insecurities and fears, but thanks to her persistence, she was eventually able to convince her husband and the bureaucrats to circumvent the de facto headscarf ban in the highest public areas of the country. It is important to remember that there was still significant opposition to Gül as president, especially in the first year of his tenure.

Once, we attended a classical music concert performed by a symphony orchestra that was under the auspices of the presidency. When Gül entered the hall, I saw a woman refuse to stand in respect like everyone else and say bitterly that he was not her president. I could not help but say that he was the rightful, duly elected president of the nation. It was this kind of lack of respect and resistance to the democratic process that made people like me take sides with the AKP. In retrospect though, today I can say that I would have respected her right to peaceful protest. I, too, had been affected by the extremely charged and polarized environment.

The first lady spent most of her time renovating the presidential properties in Ankara and Istanbul, but she also inserted herself into many other matters that were not within her purview. The president exerted almost no visible control over her. She tried hard to influence and gain the respect of the country's elites. She invited the leading industrialist families (Koç, Sabancı, Eczacıbaşı, Özyeğin, to name a few) to private dinners, especially at the Huber compound in Tarabya, Istanbul, which overlooks the Bosphorus, during the summer.

**With President Gül, Tarabya,
Istanbul, summer 2010
(Photo courtesy of presidential photographer)**

On one hot summer day in Tarabya, she gave me an "important" task. I was to organize her personal library. The difficulty was that there were no set criteria. It was mainly a matter of appearance. Or some sort of busy work to provide an opportunity to exert dominance. When she reviewed the results of my efforts, she said, "You want to work with Abdullah Bey [the president], but you are not ready. You cannot even put the books in order."

That incident pushed the limits of my tolerance and patience. I resolved to quit as soon as possible, but I would first have to survive an upcoming official trip to the U.S. The loyalist head of security, Çangal, told me that she took me along on the trip just to prove my incompetence to everyone else.

The trip to the U.S. for the U.N. General Assembly meeting in September 2010 created what are probably my worst memories of New York City and Boston. I was not the only one reprimanded by the first lady, but it was indeed almost her goal to humiliate me throughout the tour. I was always on alert because the first lady could call me at any time of the day for anything. The first couple and the inner circle stayed at the Plaza Hotel in Manhattan. The rest of the entourage was sent to a neighboring hotel. Although I was always on call, I was not part of the first group, while the first lady's personal shopper and trend follower had her own room at the Plaza. Fortunately, one of the female bodyguards shared her room at the Plaza with me to make my life—and everyone else's—a bit easier.

I had naively hoped to attend the president's meetings with media leaders, but First Lady Gül made sure I did not have time. Someone else might have enjoyed a trip to Escada on Fifth Avenue on behalf of the president's wife, but to me it was a waste of time. Sometimes we would go into stores with the president and a group of Diplomatic Security Service agents in suits and you could see that people wondered who we were. I could not help but think that no matter how much those in power puffed themselves up, beyond the borders of Türkiye, few knew or really cared who we were.

I did have the opportunity to attend a luncheon at a farm hosted by First Lady Michelle Obama for first ladies attending the U.N. session. I sat right behind Mrs. Gül to be available to translate for her if requested, but that was a mistake I should have foreseen, given what I knew of her. Though my intention was to be helpful, she apparently regarded it as making her look bad.

After the event, we got into the car. There were two American protection officers sitting in the front. She had previously complained that she did not need so much help, but now she chided me for not translating when she needed it. Apparently, First Lady Obama had said, "We live in a bubble," and First Lady Gül did not understand, but if I had intervened, she likely would have been angry. I could not win. The security agents presumably did not understand Turkish, but it was clear that I was being reprimanded by my boss. It was embarrassing, but more uncomfortable for them than for me at that point.

**With First Lady Obama and visiting first ladies, New York, September 2010
(Photo courtesy of official photographer)**

Our second stop was Boston. The nightmare got worse on the presidential plane. First Lady Gül cared a great deal about the gifts she gave and received. Since American civil servants are not allowed to accept expensive gifts, she sent only relatively modest items. I had written "tablecloth" instead of "table runner" on a note that accompanied her gift to First Lady Obama and she chastised me in front of a few ministers and high-ranking diplomats in the private section of the aircraft. I do not think First Lady Obama cared about such details, but for First Lady Gül, these things were very important.

When she asked me what I had learned throughout my education, I told her that I was a political science major and that you are not taught about home economics and decorating in graduate school. It's no wonder I would never be a favored employee.

On that flight from New York to Boston, I gave serious thought to quitting on the spot, but I was worried about the consequences. She had the power to make my life very difficult if I did not leave on good terms. Everyone around me who knew her warned me against a sudden resignation. Nonetheless, after returning from that trip, I told the president in private about my desire to leave. He listened to me sympathetically and said he knew that I was not satisfied. At first, he suggested returning to academia, but when I said that I had already decided it was not the right fit for me, he suggested the media, saying that journalism would better suit my personality, and he was right.

Though I was now eager to leave, it took a few months to ensure a smooth departure from the palace. I continued to perform my duties and the first lady generally ignored me, but one day, she scolded me after I had attended a presidential meeting, saying that the president was not happy that I was attending his events. This was clearly not the case, as I had heard the opposite with my own ears. I have to say that President Gül always treated me with respect. Aside from his disappointing political record in later years, I remember him fondly as a gentleman, a tolerant husband, and a caring father.

President Gül was very concerned about Türkiye's image abroad. During my attempt to perform tasks with more political substance, I had begun to inform him about foreign press related to Türkiye. He often regretted that there was an insufficient number of qualified people to speak to the foreign audience and address accusations made against the government. While it is impossible for presidents to be completely impartial, compared with Erdoğan and others, Gül was able to strike a reasonable balance, at least for a while.

After Erdoğan's massive corruption came to light some years later, Gül could have pushed for accountability and freedom of the media and judiciary, but he disappointingly chose to remain silent and missed a tremendous opportunity to provide historic leadership. To this day, I do not know why he was so afraid of backlash from Erdoğan. He was the only potential leader who could have challenged Erdoğan before it was too late.

My time in government taught me to view those in public office with less naiveté and strengthened my belief in the need to implement a merit-based, accountable system in Türkiye. My experience in Ankara made me realize that the Turkish bureaucracy is besieged by incompetent but clever loyalists who are often able to survive thanks to devious games. I had long thought Ankara offered no place for women, but now I believe that there is no room for idealists or simply decent people who want to work to make genuine progress. In the abyss of the Turkish state, the overwhelming majority are only concerned with advancing their own interests.

I was among the most industrious employees in Çankaya Palace. I refuse to be unassuming about this, though modesty is encouraged in Turkish culture. The

Gül family recognized that I was honest, reliable, skilled, and hardworking. Yet these were not attributes that were valued. I suffered because I was not willing to be one of the many sycophants who surrounded them.

My time in the presidency was certainly full of lessons and invaluable experiences. Titles and offices hold little inherent worth to me and are not automatically engendered with more than the required respect. I learned early on to value someone's personality and integrity more than their status.

I continue to be grateful for the opportunity, but I never felt that the Gül family did me any favors. I know that I was qualified and worked hard. I came to believe that First Lady Gül saw official positions as a kind of bounty she could distribute, and perhaps either her personality or conditions of the time prevented a more satisfactory and productive experience. I chose not to participate in the circumstances I was presented with, but I learned something about just how important the state is in the minds of Turks.

CHAPTER 12

After my discouraging experience in the nation's highest government office, I was almost sure that I wanted to work in the media, even though it was an unusual path to take. Typically, people want to move from the private sector to the public sector to have greater job security and less-demanding work hours. I, on the other hand, knew that I had to be able to speak my mind and make a substantive contribution. Yet the thought of starting a career in the media at a point later in life than usual gave me pause. In addition, people I considered mentors, such as Fehmi Koru and columnist Soli Özel, who was also my thesis advisor at Bilgi University, did not recommend that I try to become a journalist. I was counseled by many to be patient and pursue a career in the bureaucracy.

I decided to try a job at the Ministry of Foreign Affairs (MFA), since it would give me an inside look at one of the most prestigious institutions in the country. Based on my experience in the Office of the President, I knew that career diplomats were often very protective and resistant to accepting outsiders into their world, but it was the next logical option. I was encouraged to take the exam to enter the diplomatic service, but I knew that I did not want to be a diplomat; I thought it was too late and that my character did not fit the strict hierarchy and requirements of the diplomatic profession. However, I did enjoy being around diplomats.

Work with the Center for Strategic Research (SAM), an MFA think tank, offered a reasonable interim solution. I would be part of the diplomatic service, but also have the benefit of some autonomy since no one really considered SAM part of the ministry. However, as it happened, Ahmet Davutoğlu, the foreign minister at the time, wanted to increase the influence of this semi-academic institution within the ministry. As part of this effort, he appointed a bright, young professor of international relations, Bülent Aras, to head the department and rejuvenate the center. Aras assured me that I would have the opportunity to develop under his leadership. So, in late December 2010, I moved from the presidency to SAM.

Many considered this a demotion or termination and a kind of punishment. After a prestigious job working with the president, at first, a quiet position in the MFA did indeed feel a bit like a downgrade, even though it had been my decision to leave the presidency. I could not explain to anyone that the main reason for my departure was the extremely difficult character of the first lady. Her volatility and insecurities were well known to those around her, but her image in the eyes of the general public was positive. I was relieved to have some independence and a more challenging assignment at the think tank. Professor Aras was relaxed and flexible, and he gave me the space and the stimulation I needed.

I originally thought that I could pursue my unfinished Ph.D. at Bilkent while working at SAM, but when I listened carefully to my inner voice, I realized that if I did, it would be because of social pressure, not my own desire and dedication. A doctorate would have made life easier for me professionally in some ways, and I did not think it would be difficult to complete at that stage, but I just did not have the necessary commitment.

The work at SAM was not demanding, and since I was alone in Ankara, I decided to create more work for myself. I could have developed a hobby or pursued other interests, but instead, I busied myself with coordinating and conducting training programs for young diplomats, seminars, writing academic papers, and other adjunct activities.

**A Center for Strategic Research staff photo, 2011
(I am fourth from right)
(Photo courtesy of official photographer)**

In 2011, I realized that I was 32 years old and I started to worry more about being single. Most of my peers and colleagues were married. My path was still unsettled. In the large apartment in a popular residential area of Ankara that my father had rented for me from one of his friends, loneliness and renewed doubts often hit me hard. Friends arranged a number of blind dates, generally with bureaucrats, and some of the guys were really intelligent, but for one reason or another it did not work out. In retrospect, I suspect that I did not really consider these men potential partners because I was not yet truly emotionally available, despite my anxieties about being unmarried.

My hope for quiet responsibility and freedom at work was soon dashed by a consummate bureaucrat and diplomat, Oğuz Ateş, who became a supervisor at SAM. He was patronizing and controlling, micromanaging the entire staff. As I witnessed him make junior staffers print out draft emails, review them just to change a comma or some other insignificant detail, and waste hours on unnecessary tasks, I realized anew that I was not suited to the strictly hierarchical order of diplomacy. It was agonizing to see bright minds wasted in the idiosyncrasies of bureaucracy.

I knew that I was capable of working responsibly and independently, and I bristled under excessive oversight. I spoke to some senior officials in the ministry, such as Deputy Foreign Minister Naci Koru and the president's chief of staff, and after that, Ateş retreated somewhat.

To be honest, I have noticed over the years that I hate to be given orders. I have always been independent-minded. It is ironic and frustrating that I am one of those accused of delegating their will to a cleric and not making their own decisions because I sympathized with the Gülen movement. Nothing could be further from the truth. I did not hesitate to challenge the first lady or Gülen himself.

Proximity to power must lead to a certain blindness. At the time, I thought that Davutoğlu might make a good foreign minister because he was a knowledgeable professor. A chapter from his book on international relations had been required reading in one of the courses in the Bilgi master's program. He was far more educated than many others in the cabinet, and his team included many of his former students. But his inner circle was not immune to infighting and other weaknesses.

For example, I never understood how Ali Sarıkaya, who was ridiculously arrogant and clearly corrupt in my opinion, could be his closest advisor, but then I am reminded that principals demonstrate their character in all of their decisions. Years later, I learned that Sarıkaya had hired a private chef for himself, of course paid for by the state, who cooked only gluten-free meals and that he had taken ministry kitchen staff to Davos, Switzerland to provide a barbecue in the snowy Alps. Davutoğlu takes pride in claiming to not be corrupt, at least in comparison with others in Türkiye. Draw your own conclusions.

While at SAM, I once wrote an opinion piece for *Today's Zaman*. Just hours after the article was published, I had a call from Gürcan Balık, a former diplomat and a chief advisor to Davutoğlu. He told me that his job was to protect the minister and his office, and that political commentary written by an official member of the Foreign Ministry could hurt Davutoğlu. I felt uncomfortable and had the article removed online, but I realized that I could not be as free as I had thought while I remained within the state bureaucracy.

It is ironic that Balık, one who diligently tried to shield the minister, was among the first victims of the

2016 purge. His rapid rise in the diplomatic service and his somewhat vain style had earned him many enemies. He was a graduate of Fatih College, the flagship high school of the Gülen movement. But this appeared to be his only tie to the movement. He was married to a Russian woman and seemed to lead a secular life. When the government began a witch hunt against actual and alleged Gülenists, Balık was first removed from his post as ambassador and then imprisoned on coup charges without evidence.

Another brilliant diplomat, Tuncay Babalı, became the youngest ambassador at the Foreign Ministry and was appointed to serve in Canada. I remember joking with him at the time about a 25-year term, since it could have been expected that he and Balık would likely remain ambassadors until they retired at age 65. He said that his goal was not to enjoy a comfortable term in office, but to serve the nation. "I would be sad if you had such an impression of me," he said, which made me regret my jest. He, too, would later be imprisoned for alleged links to the Gülen organization.

Deniz Kılıçer was another diplomat I came to know. She was very entertaining to talk to and she was known to be a great source of gossip. She used to say that she was promoted later than her colleagues because she was a single woman, and she was probably correct in this observation, at least to some extent. One day, she said to me, "Rumor has it that you are a Fethullahist [Gülenist]." I was disturbed by the notion of possible profiling but did not worry too much about it since I had no ambition to pursue a lifelong career in the bureaucracy.

CHOICES

I did not try too hard to hide my religious practices. It was known that we had prayed in a corner of the presidential residence. I also publicly praised the Gülen movement schools that had been established around the world. Yet many others did feel it necessary to hide their religious views. Something as small as not wearing a gold wedding band was enough to be profiled as pious in Kemalist Türkiye, since Islam forbids men to wear gold.

A pleasant memory of my time at SAM was a Balkan tour we organized for new diplomats. We traveled in two buses from Ankara to Sofia, Skopje, Pristina, Tirana, and northern Greece. The Balkans were impressive and beautiful, and we all learned a lot about the region thanks to Haluk Dursun, a history professor who accompanied us. If I have the opportunity, I would like to visit the Balkan region again.

Looking back, I learned many things about the way that power and politics actually work during my time in the civil service. For example, I saw that intellect or being a good public speaker is not enough to succeed in politics. Davutoğlu could easily arouse patriotic feelings and motivate others, but his passion was due to his dreams of expanding Turkish influence in the former Ottoman territories. Türkiye was shifting from a foreign policy of "zero problems with neighbors," which emphasized trade and amicable relations, to once again expressing opinions and great interest in regional politics.

There was internal criticism, particularly of Davutoğlu's Syrian policy, but I heard it expressed publicly by only one MFA staff member, Ayşe Sözen. Her father was an old friend of Erdoğan and she came from the ranks of the AKP. Her loyalty later earned her a

145

position in the presidency with Erdoğan, and she was subsequently appointed ambassador to Oman.

As a friend, I enjoyed Sözen's company, but after witnessing the cruelty of political Islamists in Türkiye, I cannot help but think that no one can really be saved from this crooked ideology. Strikingly, Sözen frequently mentioned how worried she and her former housemate, AKP member of parliament and Minister of Education Nimet Çubukçu (née Baş), were that even they were being secretly recorded. It was not an entirely unreasonable concern. After I had left the presidential residence, I learned from a reliable source that Erdoğan had wiretapped Gül and his family, especially in the last years of Gül's term. Yet it is always the functionaries who take the fall, never the masterminds.

My experience in the state bureaucracy revealed to me very clearly that hard work and qualifications were not enough to secure and maintain a place in government. Rather, it depends on who you know, to whom you are loyal, and playing the game. This is not unique, of course, but it was a profound disillusionment and disappointment.

I had the opportunity to observe followers of the Gülen movement within the state bureaucracy. They have been accused of infiltrating the civil service with nefarious intentions but compared with many unqualified and greedy officials cozying up to those in power, the young, respectable, and highly qualified Gülen sympathizers struck me as preferable. They seemed to be idealistic, hard-working, reliable, and honest. But the opacity and solidarity of the movement alarmed outsiders. I heard people complain that those in the movement only protected one another and voice other similar suspicions and rumors. I was not then able to realize the extent to which such apprehension and gossip would be used against the movement.

Türkiye has long been vulnerable to ideological tribalism and cronyism, but when a group with a religious identity claimed more space in the state, it was perceived as a threat, especially, though not exclusively, by the secular establishment. I can say that I saw a marked and admirable difference between traditional officials and supporters of the Gülen movement. For example, the former often did not mind wasting public funds, while the latter did not want to spend taxpayers' money unduly in recognition that they would be accountable to God.

Similarly, the Gülen movement has been particularly condemned for "insinuating" followers into the police department, but I have to say there was an unmistakable improvement in the overall decency of police officers in the early 2000s, though it would prove to be inconsistent and decline in subsequent years. It should go without saying that any officers who follow unlawful orders or engage in inappropriate conduct should be held accountable, regardless of their identity. After all, power can corrupt even the faithful.

The movement was not immune to mistakes. It was a product of the environment in Türkiye and suffered to some extent from the ills of society. Any "bad apples" should have been eliminated and publicly ostracized from the movement, but I have yet to see evidence of sufficient self-evaluation in any respect among the higher echelons of the movement, though this was not apparent to me until relatively recently.

I must admit that I grew closer to the movement during my years in the state bureaucracy. I sincerely believed that these idealists could finally tame the corrupt civil service. But I did not want to try to create a career for myself within the civil service. I recognized that I was not cut out for it, and that I had put aside my passion for writing and commentary.

Contrary to the promises made by Davutoğlu and Aras, SAM was marginalized further within the MFA, including moving the center from the main building. It was very isolating and our position in the hierarchy was evident. Professor Aras was replaced by Davutoğlu's close advisor, Mesut Özcan.

By the summer of 2012, I was quite discouraged and there were no opportunities for advancement. When I told Deputy Foreign Minister Naci Koru of my dissatisfaction, he said that his hands were tied because the first lady was still monitoring my status. Once again, it was painfully obvious that there was no place for me in Ankara. Koru suggested that I work in the Istanbul office of the MFA. It was a tempting idea to be at home and have an office on the Bosphorus, but it would be nothing more than a dead-end job that essentially existed only on paper. I was too young and ambitious to accept relegation to a corner and adopt a "retirement mood." I was convinced that I had not yet reached my full potential and wanted something more.

CHAPTER 13

As I began to do some more soul-searching, I talked to the editor-in-chief of the *Today's Zaman* daily, Bülent Keneş. He had been gracious and encouraging when I had spoken with him after returning from the U.S. and just before starting at the MFA, but others had always dissuaded me from my desire to work in the media. Now, I was ready to commit. I had a meeting with Ekrem Dumanlı, the editor-in-chief of the *Zaman* daily, the prominent sister newspaper written in Turkish, and he offered me employment. *Zaman* had the highest circulation in the country, and the media group, associated with Gülen, included several other newspapers and television channels. I told Dumanlı about my desire to join the media, and when I visited him at the large, modern *Zaman* building in Istanbul, he said that they could use someone with my resume in various positions within the media group.

When I left his office, my mind was made up. I wanted to leave public service and become a journalist. My mother and others around me still thought it was a mistake to give up such a supposedly secure career for the media, but even after all that I would later go through, I have no regrets about pursuing my desire to become a columnist. In early July 2012, I resigned from the MFA, returned my diplomatic passport, and took a road trip to the Black Sea region with my family before beginning my new journey in journalism.

In Istanbul once again, I was eager and excited. I was confident that I had the potential to be a good journalist, but I was a late entrant to a career in the media. I thought that joining the staff of *Today's Zaman*, the English-language daily sister paper to *Zaman*, would be a good starting point. It was one of two daily newspapers in Türkiye printed in English at the time and had a limited yet influential readership. It was not merely a translation of the Turkish *Zaman*; it had an independent staff and editorial line, though they shared resources. I thought that my ability to write comfortably in English would help to balance my lack of experience.

On my first day at the paper, July 19, 2012, I was both nervous and excited. Keneş, the longtime editor-in-chief of *Today's Zaman*, is a passionate journalist. He was demanding, but also supportive of anyone willing to work hard. He appreciated enthusiasm and the desire to make a difference. The challenge for me was learning to write like a reporter rather than as a commentator or an academic. The editorial system and standards at *Today's Zaman* were higher than most other media outlets in Türkiye. We were fortunate to have the guidance of Keneş and Chief Copy Editor Helen Betts. Betts could be intimidating, but her professionalism and perfectionism forced us all to do our best.

I became one of the paper's most prolific reporters. I enjoyed my new job, even though I was simply a correspondent. In bustling Istanbul, there were times when I followed and reported on three events a day. We always had more stories than our relatively small team could handle. Our job was twice as difficult as the reporters at our sister paper because we were writing in a foreign language and with fewer resources. The *Zaman* team was huge, while we could hardly take a break. Aras, my former boss at SAM, asked me why I would leave the MFA to become a lowly reporter, but I was happy with my decision and this exciting new path.

It was not long before I was given additional responsibilities. I loved being a journalist, but working as an editor was a horror to me. No matter how many times I said to Managing Editor Celil Sağır that I would be of best service producing content, he would assign me all kinds of tasks, from tedious translations to page editing. It was useful experience, but it was not where my strengths or interests lay. I will always appreciate Sağır's comment during my first days at *Today's Zaman* noting that the paper did not knowingly print lies or slander. This was a regrettably uncommon stance in Türkiye's media and is often not believed.

Every Monday morning, the managing editors of both papers, as well as some columnists, met for a weekly meeting. Usually, *Today's Zaman* was represented only by Keneş or, in his absence, by Sağır. I became one of the few women present for these meetings. Dumanlı asked me to attend and contribute my opinions, and I was not shy about expressing them.

Typically, few of those at the crowded table would speak, and even fewer challenged Dumanlı. At first, I thought the attendees were simply not engaged or excited about what was happening, but later I came to think that they were probably not speaking up out of fear that Dumanlı might react strongly. I think there was some

151

element of the common culture of fear in the workplace. Keneş, however, was not afraid and frequently voiced his own thoughts.

Contrary to what many suspect, neither Dumanlı nor anyone else directed what should be written in opinion columns. Once I became a columnist, I was asked only once to remove a criticism of Russian President Vladimir Putin to protect the Gülen movement-affiliated schools in and around Russia. We regularly criticized officials and policies and presented a variety of contributor opinions, at least in *Today's Zaman*.

I put in long hours and was tired of living alone, so I did not mind living at home with my parents. I had the benefit of saving my salary for my own needs and enjoying my mother's hotel-like services, but though I was happy and doing well, I also started to feel even more concern that I was still single, unlike most of my contemporaries.

In late May 2013, I participated in a trip to Brussels for a group of journalists and academics that was organized by the Friedrich Naumann Foundation for Freedom, a German foundation for liberal politics. It was at that time that the Gezi Park protests erupted in Istanbul.

When the government announced that it would demolish and redevelop one of the few remaining parks in the heart of Istanbul, peaceful protesters resisted. I had long opposed the excessive development in Istanbul and the beloved mega projects of Erdoğan and his construction cronies, and so I sympathized with the protesters' efforts to preserve the small park in historic Taksim Square.

CHOICES

The police set fire to the tents of protesters who had refused to leave in order to prevent demolition and indiscriminately used tear gas and water cannons. The protests only grew. It was no longer simply about the park. In fact, it never had never been simply about the park, but this particular protest of the government's increasingly authoritarian and Islamist approach to governance would surprise everyone. Different factions of society unified in protest, including some pious Muslims, and supportive events occurred in cities across the country and even internationally. Erdoğan was dismissive and refused to negotiate despite widespread calls for calm. He called the protesters looters and losers. Crackdowns and violence continued for weeks.

Naturally, I disapproved of the heavy police response to peaceful protesters; however, when the protests expanded and became violent, I hesitated to support the demonstrators. I began to distance myself after Erdoğan claimed that a woman wearing a headscarf and her child had been attacked by Gezi demonstrators in the nearby Kabataş neighborhood.

Harassment of visibly devout Muslim women was not unheard of. I knew of similar incidents, such as that told by a female employee at the newspaper, who recounted that a driver had tried to intimidate her while in a secular neighborhood, and so this provocative story of contempt and discrimination, like others, also succeeded in inflaming the already shocked and upset public. Yet it was a particularly ugly, vulgar, and even ridiculous story in its details.

The tale was subsequently revealed to be false, but the damage was done. In the first days that the claims were spread about, even respected secular journalists, like İsmet Berkan and Balçiçek Pamir (née İlter), said that they had seen video footage that confirmed the account of brutal harassment. They later apologized when confronted with evidence that the story was disinformation. I never would have thought so many could lie or be misled or even coerced so easily and add fuel to the fire, but this was almost surely the intent. I was still learning many lessons.

The mainstream media response to the Gezi Park events played an important role. Initially, there was very muted coverage, largely in deference to the government, and CNN Türk was ridiculed and shamed for airing a documentary on penguins when there was violence in the center of Istanbul. Social media, however, was flooded with news and camaraderie for the protesters, as well as pro-government commentary.

Today's Zaman and *Zaman* took different editorial stances during the Gezi protests. *Today's Zaman* covered the story from the beginning, and though I think personal sentiments of the staff were mixed, at least in the early days, with some disapproving of what at first they thought were young hooligans, we did our best to report accurately. As events progressed, the paper became increasingly critical of the government. *Zaman* also slowly became more vocal as events unfolded and the significance became clearer. Gülen recommended that supporters of the movement demonstrate tolerance.

I did not actually go to Gezi Park until the violent clashes had largely subsided. When I finally got there, it felt like a festival for Erdoğan haters. Everywhere you looked there were signs, humorous and irreverent graffiti, art installations, and even food stalls, a makeshift library, first-aid and veterinary clinics, music performed on a stage, and more. Young people, families, representatives of all strata of society had taken over most of Taksim Square, which is quite large. They had also held a public fast-breaking meal that stretched for blocks. The sense of community was palpable. It was clear that the protest was the result of widespread pent-up frustration with the AKP, and particularly Erdoğan's condescending and oppressive style.

In Taksim Square, the primary site of the Gezi Park protests, 2013

I criticized Erdoğan's desire to rule everything in my *Today's Zaman* blog, but I admit to initially having missed the bigger picture. I should have been more critical of the excessive use of force against demonstrators and acknowledged what it meant. I, like others, was still fearful of the perceived threat of secularist efforts to dominate, but the government's reaction was completely unacceptable. While President Gül and others tried to resolve the crisis, Erdoğan deliberately tried to stir people up even more. This was, of course, his strategy. He did not care about the effects of increasing polarization and even violence because he believed he would profit from it.

The Gezi protests had shaken the whole country, as similar events have in other countries, but the dissent was brutally suppressed. There were many injuries and it cost the lives of protesters, police officers, and bystanders, including children. Though the demonstrations were eventually stamped out, the park was ultimately spared and the original plan for development was scrapped. There would soon be other development projects in the area, but the thought of a popular uprising so unnerved Erdoğan that public demonstrations have been strictly curtailed ever since. He blamed the chaos on covert forces and international interference.

Not long afterward, in the fall of 2013, Erdoğan made a critical decision that forever changed his relationship with the Gülen movement. Though the previously close relationship had become increasingly fraught, when the government announced that it would eliminate private preparatory schools (dershanes), ostensibly as part of a reform of the education system but widely recognized as an effort to curtail the movement's influence on education and society at large, it sparked a fierce reaction. The dershanes were the backbone of the movement; they were an important source of revenue and recruitment that also provided a valued educational service. This issue was relevant to families both secular and religious across the country who relied on these schools.

Today's Zaman reported on it extensively, perhaps even more than necessary. For the first time, the movement mobilized its base for a social media campaign. Once again, the close solidarity among members drew concern when they garnered sufficient attention for the issue to become a trending topic on Twitter (now X). However, I was perhaps guided by groupthink and overestimated the strength of the movement and their ability to impact society. It was only much later that I realized how easily you can lose in a war with the state, especially a state that does not mind destroying the lives of its own citizens.

CHAPTER 14

My longtime dream of becoming a columnist was realized in December 2013 in this tense political climate. When Dumanlı informed me that management was considering adding me as a columnist for *Zaman* in addition to my role at *Today's Zaman*, I was thrilled. Of course, I did not know that revelations exposed that same month would impact the fate of the entire country.

On December 17, 2013, Türkiye awoke to reports of the detention of numerous high-profile individuals as part of a corruption investigation that incriminated several sitting government ministers and family members, the head of a state-owned bank as well as other prominent business and political figures, and Reza Zarrab, an Iranian with Turkish citizenship who had ties to the Turkish government. Zarrab was implicated in a multibillion-dollar gold-for-gas scheme to evade sanctions on Iran. He was also connected to Babak Zanjani, an Iranian who was also soon to be convicted of embezzlement and corruption.

Large amounts of cash and expensive "gifts" were confiscated from the homes of the detainees and there were charges of bribery, corruption, money laundering, and more. At first, all of the major television and news outlets reported it, but within hours, the story was effectively buried. My very first column, which had previously been scheduled to run on December 18, was about the relationship between international transparency reports and corruption. My aspiration to become a columnist had come true at a critical time for the country and the newspaper.

On December 25, reports surfaced of additional corruption investigations, now involving one of Erdoğan's sons. In truly democratic countries, the government would suffer following such a scandal, but Erdoğan proved again to be a political wizard. When he portrayed the investigations as a coup attempt to undermine him and began to purge the police force, I thought no one would believe or tolerate such a nonsensical story. But many were indeed ready to believe—or at least accept—anything Erdoğan said, if only for the sake of stability.

Erdoğan quickly found a culprit to name and target. He claimed that there was a "parallel structure" within the state: the Gülen movement. The allegations used pre-existing fears of powerful and threatening shadowy networks and evolved into accusations of an international conspiracy, convenient bait for his adherents.

In short order, efforts to enforce the rule of law were reversed. Zarrab and others were released within months, though Zarrab would later be apprehended in the U.S. He would serve prison time there and become a government witness, implicating Turkish businessmen and others. Following the initial detentions and public outcry, Erdoğan reshuffled his cabinet, but police chiefs who led the corruption investigations were fired and jailed, as were the prosecutors. Even their families were implicated and suffered the effects of the vendetta. A parliamentary investigation was also ultimately thwarted, and all of this was still only the beginning.

Since conventional media could not be relied upon to provide a full and reliably factual account, social media platforms became alternative channels for the free flow of information, as well as mis-/disinformation. In particular, two anonymous Twitter accounts became sources of spectacular claims.

The first, posting under the pseudonym of Haramzadeler, uploaded alleged recordings of incriminating conversations relating to graft, including shocking phone discussions between Erdoğan and his youngest son, Bilal. In one recording, Erdoğan appeared to instruct Bilal to dispose of huge amounts of cash, apparently to evade unpleasant consequences of a police raid. Bilal was apparently unable to disburse the entire sum and asked his father what he should do with the remaining 30 million euros. Documents later revealed that the family decided to buy a few expensive villas on the hills of the Bosphorus with the "loose change."

A second account, identified as that of a government insider who posted as Fuat Avni, became a sensation by predicting raids and other government activity.

Miraculously, Erdoğan survived these scandals. He simply said that the recordings were fake. Many rejected this, but a large part of the population was never even aware of the whole story, and a significant portion of those who did hear of it simply believed him. As a political scientist friend told me at the time, the Turkish people had empowered Erdoğan to lie. Türkiye did not turn into a dictatorship overnight, but in my opinion, it was a pivotal moment when the government was able to use such massive corruption investigations to its advantage and portray itself as a victim of conspiracy.

Erdoğan openly waged war on anything he could associate with or blame on the Gülen movement. Media outlets, such as *Zaman*, *Today's Zaman*, and Samanyolu TV (STV), were among his primary enemies. These sources refused to be silenced and continued to report on the corruption cases.

However, as critics have noted, it is fair to ask why *Zaman* and other Gülen-affiliated resources did not give more attention to the motives and facts behind similar earlier stories when others were facing accusations of conspiracy or crime. The movement had previously had a close relationship with the AKP government, but even so, as Dumanlı often told us in editorial meetings, Erdoğan also tried to interfere with the operation of *Zaman*, calling for the dismissal of columnists like Etyen Mahçupyan because he is of Armenian descent and was critical of the government.

Zaman may have had a pro-government editorial line for a time, but at least in terms of columnists, it was by far the most diverse and democratic newspaper in the country. Yet in our divided intellectual landscape, you were often labeled and judged just for writing for *Zaman* without the accuser even knowing the content of articles.

I believe that the corruption investigations were entirely legitimate. But when media that was close to the Gülen movement virtually took over reporting on the issue, association, real or fabricated, became sufficient for retribution. The movement was believed to wield influence in the judiciary and the police, and allegations of intent to overthrow the government were repeated endlessly with all kinds of scandalous supposed links and clues. The response was an unprecedented purge of the civil service and criminal cases targeting anyone who could be remotely tied to the Gülen movement. Even if members of the police forces or prosecution teams were supporters of the movement, this was not a crime and did not warrant persecution. But much of society believed the incessant smear campaign and perceived the investigations to be an attempt to undermine or unseat Erdoğan. In the run-up to the March 2014 local elections, the movement was Erdoğan's main target and scapegoat for anything. He called the movement a "virus," spoke of penetrating the "caves" of Gülen supporters, and used even worse dehumanizing and incendiary imagery and insinuation at rallies broadcast on all major media. His supporters cheered him.

In the newsroom, we had to listen to Erdoğan's absurd and arrogant insults and accusations, and it became more and more difficult to bear, but it would soon become even worse. We were still shocked when Erdoğan verbally attacked *Zaman* reporter Ahmet Dönmez when he asked a question about corruption. *Zaman* and other critical media outlets were soon banned from covering official events. It had the desired dampening effect. Questions about corruption or anything that might displease Erdoğan were largely stifled, at least among Turkish journalists. Dönmez would later have important contributions to everyone's understanding of this period and subsequent events.

The March 30, 2014 local elections were the first test for Erdoğan after the corruption investigations. Though a determination of mayors, everyone knew that this was a sort of referendum on Erdoğan. No one expected significant erosion of his support, especially given his huge media apparatus, but critics, and especially followers in the movement, were disappointed with the results. A group of Erdoğan supporters rallied outside our newspaper office; a large, vocal, and bold segment of society had begun to consider the movement a political actor, and often an outright enemy. I can now say that they were probably right in that assessment of political involvement to some extent, no matter how wrong the smear campaign was.

The circumstances in Türkiye have never been easy for journalists, but it was already clear that the media landscape was deteriorating even further. The government had established more and more control over the information the public received. We continued to fight for what should be universal principles, but we knew that the prospects were grim. I still reported as much as I could, followed as many events as I could, and occasionally traveled abroad. Work was my whole life.

On a professional visit to Africa, January 2014

The presidential election in August was to be decided by popular vote. The opposition was divided and weak in the face of Erdoğan's machine, but the CHP, the MHP, and other opposition parties put forward a joint candidate. Ekmeleddin İhsanoğlu was an academic, diplomat, and politician who had been secretary general of the Organization of Islamic Cooperation, but the public did not know him and his somewhat mild, conciliatory demeanor did not stimulate engagement. In my columns in English and Turkish I warned that the election would be the country's last exit before one-man rule. Erdoğan won with 51.79 percent of the vote. İhsanoğlu garnered only 38.44 percent, and Kurdish champion Selahattin Demirtaş, of the Peoples' Democratic Party (HDP), who received the backing of eight left-wing parties, came in third, with 9.76 percent.

The mysterious whistleblower Fuat Avni by now had millions of followers. Every night, many people checked their social media accounts to learn what might be revealed about Erdoğan's inner circle. Sometimes there were accurate advance hints about raids, which made the posts reliable in the eyes of many. At that time, I was quite active on Twitter and along with Keneş and Sağır, I was one of an increasing number of critical voices on social media. This brought us into the spotlight, and we were often attacked online by government trolls.

Fuat Avni even followed me online, which was something of an admirable or coveted thing at the time, and I had occasional direct conversations with this mysterious online figure via private messages. I do not know why I trusted this account. In retrospect, it seems foolish to rely on anonymous reports, but I think I subconsciously felt that he might be close to the Gülen movement. Who knows? Maybe it was run by Turkish intelligence to manipulate and mislead public opinion. Some even speculated that it was run by the CIA. Nonetheless, due to the accuracy of some of the predictions and the general environment, we had already begun to expect a police raid on our newspaper and the fear only grew after Erdoğan became stronger with a commanding win in the election.

CHAPTER 15

On December 11, 2014, when I returned to Istanbul from a panel discussion in the southeastern city of Gaziantep, my managing editor, Sağır, sent a text telling me to go directly to the newspaper office from the airport. On the way there, I saw that Fuat Avni had announced an operation against critical media outlets, and I understood the urgency. Once at the office, a meeting was held and the media group's lawyers explained to us what we should do in case of a raid and detention. I felt how close and real the threat was like never before, but we still found the opportunity for some dark humor. I was the only woman in the room and commented that all the men would be in the same prison, while I would be alone in another prison. I still did not realize how brutal it would be, extending far beyond those in the room that day.

Several of us, staff, columnists, and some well-known supporters, waited expectantly for hours, but there was no raid that day, and eventually we all went home. I gave my electronic devices to someone else in an effort to secure them and prevent any attempt to plant or distort evidence, and I went to a Pilates class to try to relax after a very tense day. The Fuat Avni account reported that the raid had been postponed.

On Saturday evening, December 13, the *Today's Zaman* editor-in-chief, Keneş, called me and asked me to go to the office. Fuat Avni had announced that the anticipated raid had been rescheduled for Sunday morning. This time there was an even bigger crowd of supporters at the newspaper building. We all knew that danger loomed, and that Dumanlı and Keneş could be detained at any moment. Dumanlı convened an editorial meeting and asked everyone to work toward ensuring that the newspapers would be even better. Oddly enough, this meeting was almost lighthearted. A colleague, Levent Kenez, said that we had done nothing wrong, so there was no reason to be sad. In an ideal world this would be true, but it was, of course, well known that the government had already arbitrarily imprisoned critics.

Some famous personalities came to support us, like former soccer player Hakan Şükür, who had resigned as an AKP deputy a year before in response to the closure of prep schools and the targeting of the movement. I was surprised to see Emre Erciş, who had emerged as a critical online journalist, and I even asked him what brought him there. He said that he was there to support media freedom, but he later targeted and defamed everyone associated with the movement. It subsequently came to light that he was apparently an informant for the intelligence service. In an alarmingly not unfamiliar scenario, he would later be shot and wounded by an unknown attacker while walking down the street with his young daughter.

The Turkish media were largely silent about the expected police raid, but a former journalist and editor of the *Taraf* daily, Yasemin Çongar, asked me to write a story for *P24*, a non-profit platform for independent journalism in Istanbul, and we received several requests for comment from foreign media outlets. We got little sleep that night.

Then, at around 7 a.m., there was activity at the main gate to the office premises. We were ready; a large crowd of us met the police officers with signs that read, "Free media will not be silenced." Nonetheless, when the contingent of police entered the building, it felt like an invasion and I felt my knees shaking a little as I chanted slogans. The police soon withdrew for some reason. I believe that, foolishly yet not surprisingly, they were unable to produce the necessary paperwork. We had gained more time. Veteran secular columnist and politician Oktay Ekşi came by to show support and I was glad to see such rare solidarity. Unfortunately, it remained an exception in the years to come as events continued to escalate.

By the time the police returned at about 2 p.m., the crowd of supporters outside had grown quite large. The law enforcement officers had to make their way through a peaceful but vocal and commanding crowd to serve an order for the detention of Dumanlı as well as Hidayet Karaca, the chief executive of the Samanyolu Broadcasting Group, an organization of several television and other outlets. Numerous other individuals in various locations were also detained.

The charges were related to terrorism and defamation of the president based on a few articles, comments, and in Karaca's case, an episode of a television drama. When Dumanlı was led out of the building, once again navigating the crowd that had even brought traffic on the street to a standstill, it was very emotional. The chants and cries of support were very affecting. We knew that detention and subsequent arrest and trial could lead to significant time in prison, in addition to further danger and retribution. We said farewell, entrusting their welfare to God and knowing that we would continue to fight.

With one of the protest signs prepared before the first police raid on the *Zaman* newspapers, December 2014

There was little live mainstream media coverage or even evening reporting of the raid other than what we ourselves were able to distribute on television and social media. Though it had been widely acknowledged as likely, including by Deputy Prime Minister Arınç, many media outlets elected not to cover it as a news item, probably because they were already owned or controlled by the government, feared their own vulnerability and chose to look away rather than to defend principles of press freedom, or harbored an attitude of "they are reaping what they sowed; they deserve it."

Despite ridicule and condemnation of the lack of sufficient coverage of the Gezi Park protests, CNN Türk initially broadcast earthquake preparedness lessons from

Japan as events unfolded on December 14. There were a few later print accounts and discussions on some evening political talk shows, but by and large, given the fact that it was not unusual for media outlets to face unjust persecution and the particular circumstances of increasing acceptability of the vilification of the Gülen movement, it was not cause for outrage beyond those affected and the few who would stand up for principles.

I did, however, receive an invitation to appear on CNN International that day. I was very tired and emotionally spent, but I pulled myself together and resolved not to get emotional and provide facts in the name of accurate reporting as I went to CNN's Istanbul studio. Journalist Andrew Finkel was also commenting. He had previously worked with *Today's Zaman* but did not leave on good terms and had been critical of *Zaman*, yet he said that this was a black day for the media in Türkiye. After my appearance, I was heartened by many messages of thanks and blessings.

My appearance on CNN International after the first police raid, December 2014

In the following days, many of us, staff, readers, and supporters alike, spent a lot of time, day and night, at the Çağlayan city courthouse as well as the police headquarters on Vatan Avenue, which was notorious for ill treatment of detainees. The protests were peaceful and calm; after all, this was a group that was not used to street protests and had no desire to inflame matters, merely to draw attention to injustice.

In front of a banner in the *Zaman* lobby that says "We will not be silenced," December 2014

After a few days, the crowd unified and began to chant slogans together. I remember seeing investigative journalist Mehmet Baransu among the demonstrators. He had written numerous important stories for the *Taraf* daily, including shameful revelations related to the military. Among them, his work was key to the Ergenekon cases and curbing the power of the military, and in November 2013 he had published a 2004 ruling from the National Security Council that urged Erdoğan to eliminate the Gülen movement. Baransu was subsequently arrested and convicted on numerous charges and remains in prison today.

On Friday, December 19, 2014, Dumanlı was unexpectedly released with conditions pending trial, and we also had joyous news of the birth of his daughter. However, Karaca was held in prison. He has been behind bars in solitary confinement ever since and faces an extended sentence. Despite the exhaustion and worry, the staff resolved to do all that we could, and so the next day I went to the office, although it was my day off. Many of us worked very long hours to sustain the papers and to try to explain to the public and foreign media how such events could happen.

My personal life was diminished even further during this period of upheaval. I happily volunteered to fight for democracy and media freedom, but under these conditions, finding a life partner was next to impossible. In 2015, I was 36 years old, which was on the older side for a first marriage not only by Turkish standards, but by most standards.

Before the police raid, Dumanlı had told me he had a name of a potential match for me, and after his detention, I joked with my family that it was just my luck that he went to jail before he could set me up. I never turned down an offer for a blind date, though in truth, there were not many. Often, they were terrible, but once, when I thought I might have a second date, the guy was apparently just curious to meet me. I was somewhat well-known then, at least among our supporters and pro-government detractors.

Despite the increasing pressure on us in the months that followed, I continued to work as hard as I could. I was willing to travel pretty much anywhere, inside and outside of the country. Traveling abroad often felt like a lifeline. In January 2015, I traveled to Silicon Valley, California, as part of a journalism project funded by the Hollings Center for International Dialogue. I distinctly remember feeling free when I arrived in northern California. I was also amazed at how progressive the region was. I had a glimpse at southern California years earlier, but I was more familiar with the East Coast. Though it is famously liberal, I was still struck by the open-mindedness of the Bay Area.

I also traveled to several states on a tour to speak about the problem of media freedom in Türkiye. Thanks to the connections of local Gülen supporters in the U.S., it was not difficult to organize public events with academics and American colleagues in journalism and civil society organizations. An event held at The City Club of Cleveland in Ohio, a longstanding forum supporting free speech, was one of my first major public speaking engagements. I was nervous, but by the time I finished my tour in Washington, I was even comfortable speaking in front of congressional representatives.

During 2015, I was invited to speak at several events in the U.S., including serving as moderator for a panel discussion on women's issues at the U.N. Travel from Türkiye to the U.S. became almost routine, though we all worried about possible arrest when leaving or entering Türkiye. My travel was so frequent that my Pilates instructor asked me, somewhat suspiciously, why I traveled to the U.S. so often. Apparently, Erdoğan's propaganda that the movement secretly served U.S. interests was influential even among his opponents. There has long been some degree of belief in Türkiye that anyone with ties to the U.S. was probably working for the CIA.

I guess it was especially interesting to foreign venues to host a female professional from Türkiye who vigorously defended the role of journalism and justice. As Erdoğan increased pressure on critics and isolated the movement, fewer people were willing to speak publicly. I do not regret speaking out, but I know that at times I was too idealistic and reckless. My mother became increasingly concerned and almost begged me not to mention Erdoğan in my columns and remarks, but I felt strongly that people needed to speak up.

Meanwhile, the Kurdish issue once again came to the fore in Türkiye. Yearslong efforts had produced some delicate and fitful progress toward resolution, but remained mired in mistrust, accusations of insincerity and non-compliance with agreed upon terms, and eruptions of violence among the primary parties as well as the Islamic State terrorist group (ISIS) and other actors. The Kurds are a valuable voting bloc in Türkiye and the government was eager to present an optimistic picture of the fragile peace process.

A joint press conference with members of the government and the predominantly Kurdish HDP was held at Dolmabahçe Palace in Istanbul on February 28, 2015, with vague hints at progress. This was a fairly transparent effort by the government to appease Kurdish voters prior to the year's general election. The "agreement" would later be denied and dismissed.

The Gülen movement was accused of attempting to halt or impede the process. Hakan Fidan, then the head of the intelligence services and formerly an important member of the AKP's foreign policy team who was close to Abdullah Gül and Ahmet Davutoğlu, had been summoned to testify about his negotiations with the PKK in 2012. Because the prosecutors and police involved in the special investigation were alleged to be allied with the movement, which now tainted their efforts, this incident would become an early source of friction between the government and the movement. Fidan was quickly shielded by new legislation, but the episode was not forgotten. Fidan and the National Intelligence Organization have long been suspected of doing dirty work for Erdoğan. Among other things, the agency was implicated in supplying weapons to militant groups in Syria. Fidan now serves as the nation's foreign minister.

CHAPTER 16

That spring, as the June general election approached, the pressure on critical media, especially *Zaman*, increased. The newspaper's advertising revenue declined as Erdoğan used his campaign to further smear and demonize the movement. He accused supporters of everything from drug addiction to conducting secret wiretaps and more. His ugly rhetoric was unbearable, but his huge media apparatus and scapegoating were very powerful and convinced many. It was easy for him to leverage a variety of existing fears.

In April, there was an unexpected court decision. A judge ruled that STV executive Karaca and some 75 police officers detained in the same case were to be released. Yet just when I thought to myself that there were indeed some impartial judges in Türkiye, the ruling was voided, the judge was suspended and then arrested, convicted, and imprisoned, accused of acting unlawfully and damaging the judiciary. This act was roundly criticized, even by the CHP, which noted that there were other remedies for any alleged judicial impropriety. Sadly, such a miscarriage of justice is not unusual in the vindictive cases brought by the government.

Family members and others with no role in alleged crimes are often punished in various ways, including arrest and imprisonment, for the intimidation value. Though independence of the judiciary is often spoken of, in reality, it cannot be said to exist in Türkiye. The European Court of Human Rights (ECtHR), the Parliamentary Assembly of the Council of Europe (PACE), and many other organizations and individuals, including a few brave members of the Turkish judiciary, have publicly called out unlawful imprisonment of political opponents as well as corruption and intimidation within the judicial branch, among other defects.

Purges and accusations that could be used to malign the movement, eliminate potential enemies, and daunt any critic continued. Using classic authoritarian tools, Erdoğan repeatedly claimed that he was a victim, but that he was strong and would be vindicated. Many in the police and intelligence services, particularly those who were involved in the December 2013 corruption cases, had already been arrested and imprisoned, often with long periods of detention before trial, and continued to face new allegations of various crimes.

The Gülen movement supported some former members of the police force who ran for office as independent candidates in the June election. Among them was a former police intelligence chief, Ali Fuat Yılmazer, initially arrested in July 2014 for alleged illegal wiretapping of high-profile individuals in 2008-09. He had been involved in the Ergenekon investigations and was subsequently accused of a litany of criminal and anti-government activity. Yılmazer claimed more than once that the operations were conducted on Erdoğan's orders as part of official duties, that they were legal, and that the Gülen movement was not involved. However, he was known to be affiliated with the movement, and this association and allegations of a covert plot to damage and overthrow the government were emphasized. Just who, if anyone, directed or prompted Yılmazer's actions is unknown, at least to me, with any certainty. He may well have acted independently or in response to priorities not necessarily concerned with the Gülen movement.

Several analysts have posited that remnants of the original deep state splintered into groups that operated with their own sense of duty and motivations, but the fact remains that no one from the movement condemned Yılmazer. In July, he was arrested again for involvement in the murder of Hrant Dink in 2007. I still believe that this may have been another example of a convenient scapegoat. Unfortunately, Erdoğan also directed his ire at Yılmazer's family. His two young daughters, one of whom was serving as his attorney, were also arrested on questionable charges in 2017.

Another candidate for office that year was the jailed former police chief Yakup Saygılı, a principal of the December 2013 corruption investigations. He seemed to me to be a decent person who paid a high price for performing his duty. I wrote a column supporting him as an independent candidate simply because I honestly did not see any party worth my vote.

Support for a notorious prosecutor of the Ergenekon cases, Zekeriya Öz, was also costly. I personally have no doubt that at least some elements of the military and some civilian friends tried to undermine the elected government, but that does not justify mistakes or improprieties during investigation and judicial processes. Media affiliated with the movement took up the cases with great zeal, and though Erdoğan repeatedly claimed a sort of ownership, the perception of the movement's dastardly role solidified. Now, it was time for retribution.

In retrospect, I think it was a big mistake for the movement to publicly embrace these candidates. It only reinforced a perception of a potentially sinister association with the police and that the movement was directing investigations and crimes as part of a stealthy political plot. It almost feels as though the movement may have been misled into making poor decisions, but I know little of the decision-making and it was certainly a rather desperate time.

As the late journalist Mehmet Ali Birand had warned long before the movement became public enemy number one, it had become a victim of its all-powerful image. I think many in the movement enjoyed the idea that they had a powerful presence everywhere; however, this assumption later made the movement a very useful scapegoat because it was difficult to define who belonged to the movement and who did not, much less their role in events or what stimulated activities. The movement was much more than its sympathizers in the civil service or the media, but this is frequently overlooked and misunderstood.

Just before the June 7 election, I attended the World News Media Congress 2015 in Washington, D.C., organized by the World Association of Newspapers and News Publishers, with a colleague, Abdulhamit Bilici, to raise awareness about the issues we faced in Türkiye. Candles were lit during the opening session for journalists killed in the line of duty around the world, and the more I talked to people, the more I realized that on a global scale, though Türkiye was already known for many offenses, including status as the leading jailer of journalists, it was just one country among many experiencing a decline in democratic standards. I saw that, in the end, we would essentially be on our own. Reports and condemnation from abroad only go so far with an autocrat.

Significant election campaign issues were the weak economy; the government response to ISIS; the Kurdish resolution process and conflict with Kurds; involvement in the Syrian civil war; government corruption, authoritarianism, and failure, primarily related to the scandals of 2013, the Gezi Park protests, and a horrific mining disaster in 2014; in addition to the conflict with the Gülen movement. There was broad dissatisfaction, but the results of the election were still a surprise.

Followers of the movement, who likely voted for anyone but Erdoğan (sympathizers were not directed how to vote), were disappointed that the independent candidates they had supported failed to receive enough votes to make it into parliament, which would have also provided them with immunity from prosecution. Even if they had been successful, I do not think Erdoğan would have let them take their seats. But the results were also a disappointment for the AKP, which was denied the opportunity to pursue desired constitutional reforms to replace the parliamentary system with an executive presidency. Under the leadership of Davutoğlu, the AKP lost the majority needed to form a one-party government for the first time.

Interestingly, the Kurdish HDP had been able to comfortably surpass the 10 percent threshold, denying Erdoğan's dreams of the presidency for a while. Their success was thanks in no small part to the young and charismatic leader, Demirtaş, and his female co-leader Figen Yüksekdağ (gender parity has been a tenet of HDP leadership). However, the HDP slogan "We will not allow you to become president" and criticism of the government likely contributed to the breakdown of the Kurdish peace process and the subsequent imprisonment of Demirtaş and Yüksekdağ. They, like so many others, remain in prison to this day.

The atmosphere of tension and suspicion only grew given the unexpected outcome of the election. One day that summer, I met with *Zaman* justice reporter Büşra Erdal, who told me that members of the Ergenekon faction would try to reverse the charges against them and instead indict people like her. In fact, that is exactly what happened, and she was later convicted of membership in a terrorist organization in a vendetta wave. Even CHP deputy Sezgin Tanrıkulu publicly mentioned her case and those of others who were not released despite serving the required time in prison.

Change would also be felt at the office. On October 5, 2015, Dumanlı resigned as editor-in-chief of *Zaman*. Most of us did not know his plans, but we assumed that he went into hiding. Bilici took on the position and was immediately faced with the detention of the editor-in-chief of *Today's Zaman* on October 9. Keneş had been charged with defaming the president on social media and was released on probation pending trial, but the prosecutor's objection was sufficient for him to be remanded into custody. He was released a short time later, but there was significant concern and uncertainty.

Despite all, there was a spark of public hope for an alternative governing coalition, but thanks to the MHP, led by Devlet Bahçeli, coalition talks failed, which suited Erdoğan. The nationalist MHP has a history of alliance with the AKP, though it also frequently finds fault with its governance. A snap election was to be held in November and Erdoğan was not shy about announcing his goal. He flatly said, "Either the party gets 400 deputies in parliament or..."

Adding to the turmoil, there was a surge in terrorist attacks. On October 10, an explosion in Ankara's main train station killed more than 100 people at a "Labor, Peace and Democracy" rally, most of whom were union members, Kurds, and Alevis protesting the escalating conflict in the southeastern region of the country, as well as innocent passersby. There were severe recriminations. Among them, the HDP accused the AKP of working with non-state actors to cause unrest and regain nationalist voters, and the MHP criticized the lack of security and claimed that the unity of the country was suffering from the AKP's relationships with violent groups. The level of polarization and civil unrest was alarming. The victims of the bombing were even booed by ultranationalists during a minute of silence at an international soccer match.

Amid all this high emotion and worry, I continued to report and enjoyed producing stories and giving interviews, sometimes more than writing commentary. For instance, I traveled to the border province of Edirne to cover the growing Syrian refugee crisis with *Zaman*'s skilled chief photo editor, Selahattin Sevi.

Preventing an influx of refugees was a big concern for the EU, and as expected, Erdoğan used this as leverage. Europe essentially turned a blind eye as Türkiye slipped into despotism. I felt sorry for the millions of Syrians who had to flee their homeland and struggle to survive. I didn't think that in just one year I would become a political refugee myself.

In a major blow to media freedom in Türkiye, just days before the election, the government seized control of Koza İpek Holding, a large multi-industry conglomerate owned by Akın İpek, on suspicion of terror financing and other crimes simply because the owner publicly supported Gülen. The holding's media group consisted of two TV channels, a radio station, and two daily newspapers.

When I heard about the takeover, I rushed to their TV headquarters in central Istanbul. Bugün TV was one of the few to broadcast news and views without bias, and I was able to protest the seizure on the air. I then went to see the editor, Tarık Toros. A few opposition MPs, including Eren Erdem and Mahmut Tanal, were there as well. A crowd soon gathered in front of the building, and as the police started to force their way in using water cannons and tear gas on the crowd, Toros broadcast it live from the control room. He locked himself in to transmit until the last possible minute. The transmission on both channels was abruptly terminated while he vowed to fight for media freedom. Seeing the TV screen go black and police officers and trustees arguing with the staff felt like I was in an Orwellian world.

The non-profit advocacy group Freedom House called out the blatant political motivation behind the takeover. In part, their statement read, "The appointment of managers from pro-government media outlets to head Koza İpek's media arm makes clear that the goal is control of public debate." The U.S., the European Parliament (EP), and others also expressed concern. Though there was some support from within the country, the reaction was restrained. Fear and a lack of willingness to speak up for a Gülenist were enough to limit the response. Once again, I felt some resentment toward the Turkish intelligentsia. If more people had reacted that day, the future of Türkiye might have been different. As it was, the owner had to flee the country, forfeiting many assets. It was the beginning of the largest wave of state expropriation since the Armenian genocide in 1915. All of the Koza İpek media outlets were eventually closed and Toros also later left the country.

The results of the November 1, 2015 repeat election gave Erdoğan the result he wanted. His party was once again able to form a government on its own. According to the constitution, the president's role is to be impartial, but no one could do anything about him taking sides with the AKP. On election night, a group of Erdoğan supporters celebrated the victory in front of our newspaper building. The demonization of the Gülen movement as a terrorist organization and a parallel structure within the state had taken firm hold. As I left the office that evening with deep sadness about the state of my society, I also felt more and more disconnected from it. I had returned and resettled in my home, but that night I realized that I might have to leave soon.

As a precaution of sorts, I applied for some journalism fellowships in the U.S. I continued to work for *Today's Zaman* as a reporter and as a columnist for both *Zaman* and *Today's Zaman*. The atmosphere was tough on everyone, and by the end of November, I was burned out.

CHOICES

I had a lot of unused air miles and an invitation from a friend in Thailand, so I planned a short break.

The next stunning blow was the announcement that Keneş had resigned as the editor-in-chief of *Today's Zaman*. He was still enmeshed in a lot of litigation because he was a vocal critic of the government and a likely target for additional legal trouble. I joined the guessing game among employees about who the new editor-in-chief might be. I was surprised when Bilici, the new editor-in-chief of *Zaman*, told me that I was being considered for the job. Keneş had reportedly said that I would be a good candidate.

I had never even considered such a position. While I was dedicated and a hard worker, I did not think I had enough experience in the field. I escaped the cold and the questions of Istanbul and surrendered to the warm turquoise waters of a tropical island called Koh Samet in Thailand. I was able to temporarily let go of all the stress of the past few years, despite messages from Bilici trying to convince me to take over as editor-in-chief of *Today's Zaman*. I still dream of returning to that island, even after seeing the more famous Phuket.

CHAPTER 17

As soon as I landed in Istanbul and turned on my cell phone, I saw numerous messages of concern and sympathy. When I saw the words "detention" and "imprisonment," I was scared. Was I going to be held in custody when I got off the plane? A few minutes later, I read in the news that I had received a suspended prison sentence of 17.5 months.

Prime Minister Davutoğlu had sued me and the *Today's Zaman* management team of Sağır and Keneş months earlier for insulting him on social media. The relevant message on my account was nothing but a criticism of the prime minister for allowing suppression of the media; however, the indictment also referenced a comment left by an anonymous account in response to my post. I told the judge at the hearing that there was no reasonable basis to hold me accountable for someone else's comment. Nevertheless, the court made a decision to collectively punish all three of us.

When I arrived at the newspaper, the offer I had received to become editor-in-chief of *Today's Zaman* was already known throughout the building. I had not even accepted it yet. It was the worst possible time. It was like volunteering for more oppression. When I spoke to Bilici, he said it represented a big step forward for women like me, but I knew that a young woman would probably not receive such an offer under other circumstances. I accepted, but I told Bilici that I had applied for fellowships in the U.S. and that I would go if I were to receive one. He agreed.

I started in my new position on December 7, 2015. Naturally, I was nervous about the reactions of my colleagues. I knew that some might resent the decision and it was a big risk to take on such a task when the threat of a police raid or worse was so real and imminent. Frankly, I found it more difficult to lead the staff than to produce the newspaper. I had never wanted to lead people. I was happier reading, writing, researching, and reporting all by myself. Still, I did my best under increasing government pressure. It was like working with a sword over your head. I tried to listen to all of the concerns of the employees and be as tolerant and understanding as possible.

There were times when I felt at a loss, but overall, I don't think I let anyone down. It was a difficult time for all of us. Bilici was doing everything he could to cut expenses across the media group. Advertising revenue was dropping each day and circulation was down given the stigmatization promoted by Erdoğan. I reduced the number of pages in the Sunday edition to lessen the workload on staff and some measure of costs.

The closure of the newspaper was more a question of when than if, but there was a sort of denial and perseverance as we labored to carry on. In editorial meetings, I often said that the country was becoming more and more of a hell for us and that it would only get worse. It appeared that sooner or later the need to go abroad would be inevitable, at least for those who were more visible in public.

On Friday, March 4, 2016, the time had come. That afternoon, the newspaper's lawyer sent the executives an email with a court ruling stating that our media group supported terrorist activities and would be managed by trustees. This was a euphemism for government seizure. The news went viral on social media at about 2 p.m. The day's editions were still a work in progress, but we knew that the police could arrive and stop the printing at any time. So, we decided to publish *Today's Zaman* early with half-finished pages. I directed the creation of our last independent front page with our graphic designers and copy editors. It read: "Shameful Day for Free Press in Turkey: Zaman Media Group Seized."

Creating the final front page of *Today's Zaman* before the government takeover, March 2016

After the paper went to press, the situation became even more feverish. I answered countless questions from international media representatives. I only remember one

Turkish radio host, Yavuz Oğhan, calling to get details for a report on the developments. The other media outlets were shamefully silent.

We spent most of the day waiting on the fourth floor, the newspaper's executive floor. Once again, our loyal readers and other supporters gathered in front of the building. Some opposition MPs, including Gürsel Tekin, Enis Berberoğlu, Mahmut Tanal, and Barış Yarkadaş, came to defend media freedom. Berberoğlu, a former journalist and CHP deputy, was sentenced to five years in prison for his role in releasing what were deemed state secrets by publicizing images of what appeared to be weapons allegedly shipped by the National Intelligence Organization to Syrian rebels. *Zaman* Editor-in-Chief Bilici and I spoke to the crowd outside the office. Bilici called the court decision a "black day for democracy" in Türkiye.

**Speaking to supporters at the *Zaman* office
Istanbul, March 4, 2016**

This time, when the police showed up, they were accompanied by anti-terrorist units with armored vehicles.

Shortly before midnight on March 4, police officers violently dispersed the peaceful crowd with water cannons and tear gas, broke through the main gate of our office complex, and forced their way in. It was still almost surreal to see anti-terrorist units occupying a newspaper building. When they reached the fourth floor, they cordoned off the main rooms and did not let me or Bilici in. Several of us remained in the large hallway. Tarık Toros was again broadcasting about intervention from inside, but since there was no flow of information to us, I activated Periscope, a live broadcasting application, to share the scene with the world, speaking in both Turkish and English. A police officer became angry and forcefully took my phone. When I protested loudly, I was able to take it back, but they did not allow me to use it again. One officer said, "Sweep the women off this floor!"

Two female officers grabbed me by the arms to remove me from the area. My mother told me later that

Riot police use tear gas on the crowd outside the *Zaman* headquarters, March 5, 2016 (Photo courtesy of Selahattin Sevi, *Zaman*)

she almost fainted when she saw me held by the police officers on TV. Although I did not touch anyone, one policewoman claimed that I physically resisted. When I saw photo editor Selahattin Sevi with a bleeding wound, I thought I had better go back to my office on the third floor.

They used so much tear gas outside that the effects were felt inside as well. It was all a very shocking experience. Until that time, I had not cried, but when I spoke live by telephone to a small TV station called Can Erzincan that was critical of the government, I could not help but become emotional as I described the events. The police eventually forced us to leave the building at around 2 a.m.

When I arrived home, my parents expressed their fear and said that it might be a good idea to leave the country until things "get better." That night, I also spoke with Ali Halit Aslan, *Zaman*'s longtime Washington bureau chief and a friend I trusted. He advised me to leave as soon as possible because as a senior staff member I could be arrested. I knew he was right, but without his encouragement, I might have waited. His words were an eye-opener.

The next day, Saturday, was my day off, but I went to the newspaper office. Everyone else did, too. Bilici and some others had been immediately fired by the trustee administration. The editorial offices were still occupied by the police and the building was in total chaos. Employees were allowed to enter only after a long identity review. I knew that I could not work under the trustee administration, composed of government loyalists with no relevant experience and a mission to turn the papers into government mouthpieces until the remaining resources of the media group were drained.

I didn't even want to talk to the trustees. I asked Managing Editor Sağır to be the spokesperson for *Today's Zaman*. I requested that my name be removed as editor-in-chief because I did not want to be part of a censored newspaper. The trustees quickly removed columnists whose names they knew, but probably for lack of sufficient knowledge of English, some critical articles remained in the Sunday edition. *Zaman*, printed in Turkish, was immediately turned into a pro-government paper and *Today's Zaman* would soon follow. The building already felt like a funeral home; the staff was nervous, and an air of uncertainty and tension hung heavy.

On Sunday, I again went to the office as usual, with a lot of unanswered questions swirling in my head. Everyone was worried about the future. We knew that the likely lifespan of the entire media group was limited, even as pro-government entities. I had previously booked a flight for the next day to Brazil to attend a panel discussion, but should I go?

I discussed it with Bilici and he advised me to skip the event in Brazil and consider going to Brussels, where *Zaman* had an office, if I felt the need to leave the country. As a precaution against confiscation, some of the company's assets had been sold to a partner in Belgium. I had always thought that if I went into exile, I would go to the U.S., but Belgium offered a reasonable temporary option from which to do what I could to publicize the conditions in Türkiye.

The circumstances were awful. In addition to the trusteeship, the continued presence of police officers and

CHOICES

their vehicles surrounding the building was infuriating and depressing. I decided to go to the hair salon during my lunch break to try and make myself feel a little bit better, and then, rather than go back to the office, I went to a friend's house and told her that I was considering leaving. She asked me what I was waiting for and suggested that I go as soon as possible. She even looked for the soonest flight to Brussels.

There was a flight that evening at 7:10 p.m., less than 6 hours away. I bought a ticket with award miles and drove straight home to pack and leave. On the way, I called the newspaper's finance manager and told him I was leaving. He asked if I needed money. Fortunately, I had kept my savings at home in cash for just such an emergency, knowing that the government could freeze my bank accounts, as it eventually did about a year after I left. I did not notify anyone else of my impending departure in order to avoid anything that might prevent me from going to the airport.

At home, I had the difficult task of telling my mother that I was leaving within hours. She was deeply saddened, but we both felt it was the best thing to do. We knew that travel might be prohibited or my passport canceled, as had happened to others, and that imprisonment was very possible. Two of my sisters helped me pack, but I later realized that we made some nonsensical decisions about clothing and so on. I did not even have time to say goodbye to my father, one of my sisters, or anyone in the extended family. I wanted to avoid an emotional scene, and so did not want my mother to go to the airport. In a whirlwind, my youngest sister dropped me off with just a quick goodbye.

Leaving my home country for possibly the last time, Istanbul, March 6, 2016

It was gloomy and rainy that Sunday evening of March 6, 2016. It is a date I'll never forget. It was the end of my life as I knew it and the start of a second life. I was convinced that there was no longer a future for me in Türkiye. I felt forced to leave my home and all that was most important to me. Rationally, I had long been aware of the many failures and deficiencies and the brutal consequences that can follow, and I was, perhaps oddly, not devastated to leave. I think I was in a state of something resembling shock, but it was nonetheless an emotional moment as I contemplated my circumstances. I also knew that there were many who were not as fortunate as I had been. And worse was still to come.

I did not cry, primarily because I was quite nervous until I got through passport control. While waiting, I was reminded of the film "Argo" and the hurried, clandestine departure of U.S. embassy staff from Iran after the Islamist takeover in 1979. Here I was, also fleeing and fearing the worst. It was still a strange feeling to be so apprehensive waiting for official approval at passport control, especially at home. After what seemed like a long wait, the officer finally stamped my passport and let me go through. I was relieved, but some unease remained. I was restless. Other passengers were enjoying the delicious food in the posh Turkish Airlines lounge, but I was not interested in food and anxiously awaited boarding and departure. My thoughts lurched between fear and hope.

Once aboard the aircraft, I looked out the window through the rain and wondered when I would be back. I knew it was not going to be anytime soon. I was, then as now, unable to make any prediction. I was incredibly disappointed in the people of my country. I recognized that if the *Zaman* building had gone up in flames the night of the police raid, many would have cheered, even given the many lessons of history, such as the 1993 Sivas massacre, when a mob of Sunni Muslim locals set fire to a hotel where Alevi intellectuals had gathered for a conference and festival and more than 30 people burned to death. I felt that all too little had changed.

When I had returned home after studying in the U.S., I had believed in an imminent possibility for change. I was wrong. On that day in March 2016, I knew that my life had taken yet another turn. I had to put Türkiye behind me. I was sad, but I gave a sigh of relief and thanked God as the plane took off. Anything could have happened, but I was fortunate enough to leave without difficulty.

CHAPTER 18

By the time I landed at Brussels Zaventem Airport, I was exhausted. It had been a very long and trying few days and I had no idea what to expect. The future was completely unknown. But I knew that I was free.

I called the *Zaman* Bureau Chief in Brussels, Selçuk Gültaşlı, to inform him of my arrival and a young couple, Merve and Rıza Doğan, came to pick me up. They told me that Selahattin Demirtaş, of the Kurdish opposition party, had been on the same flight. He was also under mounting pressure, but he still had political goals in Türkiye. He probably knew that Erdoğan would eventually put him in prison, but I imagine he considered it an expected consequence of his struggle as a Kurd with political aspirations. His remarkable success and popularity had made him a significant threat to Erdoğan and others who could not stomach Kurdish rights. In May, the parliament revoked the parliamentary immunity for several HDP politicians and Demirtaş, the "Kurdish Obama," was indeed arrested some months later.

Merve and Rıza took me to their apartment for dinner, but I could not really think straight. Everything had happened so suddenly and created a strange vacuum. It would take some time to find my feet. *Zaman* Belgium had arranged for a hotel room, and early the next morning, someone from the newspaper brought me to the local office. It was very humble compared with the large, modern facilities, complete with printing press, that we had enjoyed in Istanbul, and I felt the scope of the loss even more keenly.

In the following days, I talked to media representatives from all over the world about the lack of press freedom and the retribution exercised in Türkiye. A team from the Netherlands came to interview me, as well as an Al Jazeera team from London. I also appeared on Becky Anderson's CNN show *Connect the World*. I talked so much that my voice became hoarse.

Very soon, my departure also made headlines in my home country. Government trolls, including the extremely corrupt and shameless Ankara Mayor Melih Gökçek, spread lies, cruel insults, and misinformation. The secular *Cumhuriyet* newspaper, which, among other unjust abuses, had two of its senior editors arrested on charges of aiding an armed terrorist organization and publishing material that threatened state security, incorrectly reported that I had already asked for asylum in Belgium. It was disappointing, but not surprising that events were misrepresented and manipulated. Much of the Turkish media has long relied on sensationalism and social media is now widely used to defame and intimidate. I was more concerned with making my voice heard in the rest of the world.

On March 9, *The New York Times* asked me to write an opinion piece about the police raid on our papers. I titled it "Recep Tayyip Erdoğan's Despotic Zeal." The personal attacks on social media grew even more ugly and more frequent.

The following week I was a guest on the BBC program *HARDtalk*. Knowing the nature of the program, billed as hard-hitting in-depth interviews with figures involved in current affairs, I knew the questions would be tough and that the host, Stephen Sackur, would likely be provocative. I believe that probing, even antagonistic, inquiry can be appropriate and useful.

My experience, however, suggested to me that Sackur had a preconceived opinion. Rather than conducting a probing examination of the facts, I felt that he was somewhat hostile. He seemed to be dismissive of my responses to accusations, including noting that *Zaman* had already acknowledged the mistake of earlier excessive support for the government and lack of sufficient support for independent journalism when others were targeted by the government. He used the court order against the newspapers as evidence to justify retribution and legitimized the attack on the Gülen movement.

I suspect this biased view was, at least in part, a result of insufficient background research or bias. He appeared to have a firm suspicion of Gülen's motives and activities, and expressed the view held by many secularists that this was a case of "What goes around, comes around." In other words, that we deserved to be mistreated. He was not interested in the details of our case or the realities in Türkiye. Those in the movement were not the only ones suffering from the government's efforts to exert control and there were bigger issues to discuss, but he seemed to want to conform to a script he had in mind. Sadly, some degree of this careless, sensationalist "journalism" is not unusual; however, it should be noted that I am not alone in my appraisal; others have also accused Sackur of similar disregard and recklessness.

I believe that the preconceptions of Westerners are often the result of contact with limited and prejudiced resources. They often only hear one side of the story, usually secularist, but also Kurdish, for example, and form a view without recognition of the broader landscape and history. Later, I saw Sackur interview the secular Turkish journalist and author Ece Temelkuran. It was almost as if Sackur was having a nice conversation with a friend over four o'clock tea.

I felt that because of my sympathy for a religiously motivated movement, I was not considered an individual, let alone a journalist, even by some Westerners. To many, I represented a group and was defined by it, no matter my personal activities or views. Interestingly, Temelkuran also soon made the decision to leave Türkiye, which had prompted some sneering in my interview, and in a subsequent appearance with Sackur, she also seemed to be somewhat annoyed by the questioning.

My appearance on the BBC program *HARDtalk* from Brussels, March 2016

SEVGİ AKARÇEŞME

It was a very difficult time for me. I was somewhat traumatized and floundering. I felt the injustice and uncertainty that surrounded the movement and the country as a whole very deeply. I carried on, but neither I nor my mother could talk on the phone for long because we would wind up crying.

After staying in the hotel for a few days, the editor-in-chief of *Zaman* Brussels, Mete Öztürk, informed me that in recognition of the deteriorating situation in Türkiye, he had rented an apartment for the use of friends in situations like mine. On my first evening in the apartment, located in the Evere district, I had a sudden realization. I was once again all alone abroad, but this time in exile, and I did not know what to do.

A sense of despair and unfairness filled my heart. I had tried to do everything right; how could things have gone so wrong? And now what was I supposed to do in a strange city with unknown prospects? In the following days, I tried to find an answer to this question. After Gültaşlı and I insisted, the last head of *Zaman*, Bilici, also came to Brussels. He resisted the idea of leaving Türkiye so as not to leave his colleagues and friends behind, but what was the point of waiting to be further harassed or worse in a country where there is no independent judiciary? Even if not imprisonment, passports could be annulled, and futures easily destroyed. He also had a family to consider.

After his arrival, I met with Bilici, Gültaşlı, and Süleyman Tiftik, a senior follower of the Gülen movement I met in Brussels, to talk about our options. Bilici wanted to continue our struggle from Belgium, given that we had an office there, albeit with very limited resources. Gültaşlı suggested a base in London, since that was a center of European media. I thought that if I could not go to the U.S., at least an English-speaking country would be better for me. Even grocery shopping in bilingual Brussels was frustrating for me without the needed language skills. We discussed the pros and cons of the two countries, but I think we all felt lost and unsure of how to proceed.

CHAPTER 19

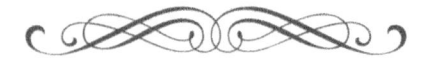

In March 2016, Türkiye also learned of the arrest of Reza Zarrab in the U.S. The government corruption scandal had not been completely buried and Erdoğan's headache was not over. He would ultimately emerge essentially unscathed, but it was a continued source of concern for some time and the government tried hard to make the case involving the state-owned bank disappear and avoid potentially damaging revelations of corruption and other unflattering activity.

Just as we were recovering from the initial shock of exile and trying to evaluate the situation, Tiftik told me and Bilici that Gülen wanted to see us. Since I had little else to do at the time but talk to members of international media and preferred to be in the U.S. rather than Belgium anyway, I accepted the invitation.

The morning that Bilici and I were on our way to the airport, there was a terrorist attack in Brussels. The city's airport was temporarily closed. Gültaşlı drove us to Paris the next day, and Bilici and I flew to New York. Bilici seemed even more perplexed than I was. I was single and childless; people with families naturally had additional concerns. At that time, he believed that we could continue to report about Türkiye from abroad. I doubted that this would be sustainable in the long run, but I wanted to try and do what we could.

Zaman's New York correspondent picked us up at the airport and drove us to Saylorsburg, Pennsylvania, where Gülen has lived at a secluded compound for years. He is reclusive and suffers from poor health. I had first seen videos of Gülen while I was at college. My roommate in the Bilkent dorm during my first semester, Nuray Yurt, and I had talked for hours about the movement. Like any young, opinionated student, I thought I knew quite a lot and did not need anyone's guidance to be a good Muslim. But as I just casually started to read some of Gülen's books, I realized that he was no ordinary preacher.

Unlike traditional religious scholars, he related his teachings to science, sociology, and history. To my way of thinking, it was reasonable that he also had ideas on political issues and current events, but even then, I did not like seeing some sympathizers in the movement completely adopt his ideas as correct without giving them due consideration.

I have always remained somewhat detached, but I have had friends in the movement for many years. I made my first visit to the Gülen retreat center in Pennsylvania while I was at Temple University, probably in 2004. A relative of my roommate, Şeyma Aslan, ran what was called a camp. This is a reference to the campsite gatherings that took place in the early days of the movement. Recounting history and learning from senior representatives of their experiences is an important part of the movement's ethos. Shared memories and experiences enhance unity and sense of purpose.

The Pennsylvania camp site was a modest facility with cottage-style houses. We spent a weekend there reading and working on our spiritual development. I remember listening to a sermon Gülen gave in the main building from a seat reserved for women. I did not meet him at that time, but it was a noteworthy experience. The first time I actually met Gülen was in 2010 while employed at the presidential palace. It was just a brief encounter. I do not want to exalt him, or any individual, but I did feel that he had a sort of aura or remarkable presence. It was not charisma in the usual sense. He did not talk much; he was friendly, yet very reserved. Until I read journalist Cüneyt Özdemir's first impressions of Gülen from about the same time, I thought I might have been positively biased because of groupthink, but everyone who met him was inspired, or at least said that they were. He was clearly not a traditional imam. In fact, I felt that he loved not only participants in the movement or Muslims in general, but all of humanity. I remember thanking him for his time and telling him about my intention to leave the state bureaucracy. He suggested that I pursue an academic career in the U.S. It could be said that this kind of advice refutes accusations of a single-minded goal to infiltrate the administration of the Turkish state.

A few years later, I met Gülen again with a group of employees from the *Zaman* media group. I was among the very few women who were offered the opportunity to go on the trip. We were not there as journalists; it was a retreat. When he met with us, I was probably the most talkative member of the group. There was no rule or warning not to talk to him, but for some reason, even the most gregarious people were largely silent around him.

CHOICES

In March 2014, I visited Gülen again with a group of women. He asked each of us to introduce ourself and then we told him about a panel discussion we were to participate in that had been organized as a side event at a U.N. commemoration of International Women's Day. A leading businesswoman, Figen İsbir, who had nothing to do with the movement, told him that many secularists in Türkiye believed that he was ruling the country with Erdoğan, especially after he had asked for support for Erdoğan in the 2010 referendum. "You are correct in your observation; we made a mistake," Gülen said.

I complained to him about the role of women within the movement and in Muslim societies. He began to discuss the Prophet Muhammad's wife, Aisha, who led an army, but his response and our visit were cut short by visitors from Kenya. There was always a long line of people who wanted to see him.

Though he lives a cloistered life, Gülen frequently receives visitors from around the world. His guests are not limited to sympathizers of the movement. In fact, meeting him was long considered a sign of prestige or power, including among those in the ranks of the AKP government. Many proudly posted photos with Gülen until the movement was declared an enemy.

I had also seen Gülen a few other times. During my trips to the U.S., I always stayed with my friend Nuray in New Jersey. On one occasion, on my way to Arkansas for a panel discussion on extremism, I mentioned the earlier question about the role of women and the lack of a satisfactory response. He confessed that he had not been prepared for the question. Gülen struck me as extremely humble, and at least he seemed to care.

SEVGİ AKARÇEŞME

When Bilici and I met with him in April 2016, it was not long after the police raid on *Zaman*. Gülen was visibly sad, and the mood was solemn and somber. Bilici told Gülen about the debates among us on how to proceed with our journalistic efforts. We were unsure of what to do. Bilici was still in favor of working from Brussels, and Gülen noted that it was the center of the EU, which meant it could be a good choice. During that visit, I told Gülen that I was frustrated with Türkiye and he said that he had never once been angry with the country, only disappointed. This was somewhat remarkable, given that he had faced persecution, but his attitude was interesting and instructive.

My friend Nuray and I saw Gülen again that spring on what would be my last visit to his compound. During our conversation, he told me that I had a God-given gift for writing and that I should make the most of that ability. I also remember him saying that he often cried for his homeland. The general mood was still one of sadness and conversation was limited.

Overall, I had always thought Gülen's message on the importance of education and service was beneficial and essential to the progress of the nation. Most of all, I was amazed at his ability to motivate people to work toward great and ambitious goals. In a country often divided into Islamists and secularists, it seemed to me that Gülen offered an alternative. I thought he offered an approach for us to move forward together. However, it was complicated. The secularists always suspected that the true goal of the movement was to establish a theocratic system in Türkiye.

I do not know if there was an end goal beyond what was preached overtly. My views, especially about the movement's leading cadres, have changed over the years, and I wish I had been more skeptical about the parts I did not know, but I acted on what I saw. Throughout my experience with the movement, I encountered people who were reliable, sincere, and made significant sacrifices for the common good. In such a large movement, of course there were some who behaved poorly, but I can still say that the people I knew from the movement were among the best I have known in my life. They genuinely wanted to do good.

Bilici and I, along with *Zaman*'s representative in Washington, Ali Aslan, were also hosted by the Committee to Protect Journalists (CPJ) in New York for a discussion on media freedom and the conditions in Türkiye. In addition to a defense of rights, Aslan was notably vocal about the need for self-criticism and admitting to past mistakes.

While in the U.S., I visited with old friends and tried to figure out what to do. Gültaşlı told me that they were working on a Belgian residence permit for me and others. I wanted to stay in the U.S., but my visa only allowed me to remain in the country for a short period. I had to return to Belgium. I could not help but think about my return from the U.S. after graduation. If I had stayed then, my life might have been more normal. Instead, I was facing a new start alone and in exile. This seemed incredibly unjust. I felt a lot of frustration and self-pity for some time.

That spring, I also reconnected briefly with a Turkish-American man I had met at a conference in Geneva a few years earlier. We kept in touch, and on paper, he seemed like a good fit for me, but he was one of those guys who was elusive. It was part of my pattern that the more unattainable a man seemed, the more attracted I was. Fortunately, I later realized with the help of therapy that I had been subconsciously choosing men who were not right for a relationship.

In May, the movement was officially labeled the "Fethullahist Terror Organization" (FETÖ) in Türkiye. Though the name and accusations of terrorist activity had already been applied to us frequently, an official designation, however unmerited, was significant and gave the government authority for its persecution.

Also in May, Prime Minister Davutoğlu was forced to resign when Erdoğan wanted to replace him with a more loyalist puppet. Davutoğlu nonetheless decided to sue me and my *Today's Zaman* colleagues Sağır and Keneş for a little over $500 in damages related to the earlier lawsuit. I would not have paid him a penny, but the judgment was collective and because there were still some connected to the case who were at risk in Türkiye, I sent my share. It was only after we paid that the case against us was closed.

In the summer of 2023, the Constitutional Court ruled that our rights had been violated and the illegitimate suspended sentence I had received was finally voided. I would like to get my money back from Davutoğlu, no matter how small the amount, but it's not worth the trouble. It's ironic that now he is in the opposition. Davutoğlu will be remembered with shame, like others who were used by the dictatorship.

CHAPTER 20

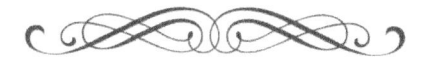

Back in Brussels, I felt isolated and stuck in a place I did not want to be. On the first day, I cried and felt sorry for myself. Fortunately, I was invited to various professional events and managed to keep myself occupied. Once, I flew to Bangkok for a speaking engagement, and as I had some time on my hands, I decided to explore the famous island of Phuket. As I watched the hustle and bustle of Southeast Asia, I was reminded once again how Westernized my mindset was. I thought that if European or American options became unaffordable or untenable, I might consider Asia or Africa as a place to live. It was like trying to walk without gravity as I struggled to find a way to regain balance and feel secure.

My Schengen visa was about to expire and finding a solution to my status soon became a real emergency. *Zaman* Brussels had been closed, but Öztürk, the editor-in-chief, set up a small company with the help of a Turkish businessman I did not know in order to continue our work and to assist me and another former *Zaman* journalist, İsmail Kavak, with residency and work permit requirements. The three of us shuffled from one local government office to another to resolve the paperwork prerequisites. Without Öztürk, who was born and raised in Belgium, we would have been lost.

The bureaucracy was slow and painful, and everything was in limbo. I applied for a U.S. visa, but I also needed a place to return to. After several visits to the Evere municipality offices, I was eventually able to obtain

My Belgian residence permit

a one-year residence and work permit with an expensive expedited application. I hoped I would not have to deal with the grouchy officials again.

In Belgium, I was free from oppression, but had other challenges to face. I was also extremely lonely. That year, I faced one of the most difficult Ramadans of my life. Fortunately, almost every evening there was an invitation from a local Turkish family to join them for the breaking of the daily fast (iftar), but the extremely long days of fasting alone in Brussels, far from all I knew and feeling adrift, were often difficult and I found myself disheartened rather than fulfilled by my faith.

I went to the office every day to make whatever contribution I could and keep busy. Some of our friends who had been dismissed from *Zaman* but were still in Türkiye had started two small newspapers, probably with funds raised by the supporters of the movement. I wrote biweekly columns for one of them, *Yeni Hayat*, but I feared that the regime would not allow them to survive. I also began to work without pay for an extremely modest news blog called *Turkish Minute*, created as a kind of replacement for the now-closed *Today's Zaman*. I wrote articles and supervised two junior reporters in Türkiye, but the news and the conditions were difficult. I spent much of my time in my apartment in Evere feeling miserable and I suffered from frequent migraine attacks.

One day in June 2016, I had a call from Rebecca Harms, a former leader of the Greens in the EP. I had earlier received an email invitation from the parliament to speak at an event about Türkiye. Another exiled journalist, Can Dündar, of the *Cumhuriyet* newspaper, and former editor of the *Taraf* daily, Yasemin Çongar, were also scheduled to speak. But apparently Dündar did not want to appear on a panel with me and my invitation was rescinded. Harms, who is a human rights advocate, seemed embarrassed, but I was not surprised by Dündar's behavior.

When Dündar was unjustly imprisoned for his reporting, I was one of the *Zaman* journalists who went to Silivri Prison to demonstrate solidarity for the sake of shared principles, but he either did not know or did not care. He had previously shown support when Koza İpek Holding was confiscated and spoke of unity and principle, but he has also expressed contempt for and distrust of the movement. In a sad irony indicative of the nonsensical nature of many of these cases, he was later described as a member of the manufactured "FETÖ" and appeared on the wanted list of terrorists. Both Dündar and Çongar have been unjustly convicted of crimes based on their reporting.

Meanwhile, the witch hunt in Türkiye continued, just as Erdoğan had promised. He did everything he said he would do to try and destroy the Gülen movement, affecting the lives of millions of people. Others not even affiliated with the movement were also targeted.

Not surprisingly, on July 1, the government blocked access to the two fledgling newspapers, *Yarına Bakış* and *Yeni Hayat*, run by dismissed *Zaman* employees, amid many other severely punishing moves.

The future was still full of unknowns and my life was in turmoil, but a small miracle happened. With the help of a recommendation from the CPJ, I was awarded a scholarship from the City University of New York for a one-year journalism program. I had my longed-for ticket to the U.S.

I received my J-1 visa for the U.S. in June, but I decided to delay my departure until late July in order to spend some time with my mother. I had no idea that events would make this a consequential decision. Just one day before my mother flew to Brussels, there was a bombing at the primary international airport in Istanbul. ISIS claimed responsibility for the attack. Türkiye had long been suspected of being a safe haven for jihadists on their way to Syria and providing other assistance, and to many, the decrease in security was the price of indifference to ISIS and other terrorists inside Türkiye.

Unfortunately, life offered me and all of Türkiye a particularly bitter surprise on July 15, 2016. I had been convinced that life in Türkiye would never be the same

CHOICES

after December 2013, and then on March 4, 2016, life as I knew it was over for me, personally. Little did I know that the future held even worse in store.

CHAPTER 21

On July 15, 2016, my mother and I were in Switzerland. I had rented a car and we had driven from Brussels to Lake Lucerne to take a break and enjoy the beautiful surroundings and refreshingly cool weather. That evening, after we had returned to our quiet old hotel, I saw strange videos and messages posted on Twitter. A soldier on the Bosphorus Bridge in Istanbul was telling people that the military was taking over. It was almost unreal, as if it were a scene from a movie, but it was also profoundly uncomfortable because I knew it just might be real.

The traffic was still heavy in Istanbul that Friday night, and oddly, soldiers on the main bridge between Europe and Asia had closed the route in one direction, stranding many commuters and creating a traffic logjam. But this was the least of what was to come. At first, it was somewhat unclear what was happening and I was anxious to learn more, but my only source of information was social media. There were soon reports of explosions and other use of force. I tried to follow as much as I could on my phone screen and I worried. Once it was clear that this was nothing ordinary, I knew that the Gülen movement would be blamed, and that the persecution would only increase.

Tanks rolled, troops stormed various locations, took hostages, including commanding officers of the military, and shocked citizens saw a statement read on state-owned TV indicating that the armed forces had taken over the administration of the country "to reinstate constitutional order." An alleged junta within the Turkish Armed Forces called the Council for Peace at Home, a reference to a famous phrase used by Atatürk, "Peace at home, peace in the world," claimed to be taking power. Erdoğan was accused of eroding democracy, secularism, and the nation's status. The truth of the existence of this council was one of many elements that quickly came under suspicion. While on the one hand, such sentiment was entirely plausible, many also saw it as another example of fabrication and misdirection.

Erdoğan was on vacation in the south of the country, but via a video call to a CNN Türk presenter he urged the public to take to the streets in defiance and vowed that the coup attempt would not succeed. In a remarkable note, imams issued calls for resistance from the mosques, and people quickly responded. Erdoğan was able to leave his holiday villa shortly before a unit of special forces arrived, presumably to capture or kill him. It was all very odd and unlike a traditional coup attempt.

In Istanbul and Ankara there was chaos and confusion as military helicopter gunfire, fighter jets, and tanks attempted to fulfill their missions. The parliament building was bombed. Civilians were killed. There was also activity in other cities that had military installations. Prime Minister Binali Yıldırım made a statement to indicate that the "illegal attempt to take control outside the chain of command" was under control and blamed the Gülen movement for the plot, noting that it would be suppressed, even if that should mean fatalities. Interestingly, a couple of years later, Yıldırım openly called July 15 "his least favorite project."

When Erdoğan arrived in Istanbul in the early hours of the morning, he called the coup attempt a "gift from God." His son-in-law, who was a cabinet minister, seemed extremely relaxed sitting next to him, given the circumstances. Erdoğan continued to rally supporters, and not long afterward there were reports that the attempted putsch was collapsing. Soldiers began to surrender, but there was continued confusion and violence in the streets. The dawn revealed that the attempt had been very poorly executed and unsuccessful, but nearly 300 were killed and thousands injured before the bloodiest coup in the country's history was over.

Analyses of the events revealed many details that raised questions. For example, the head of national intelligence, Hakan Fidan, had apparently discovered the plot before its implementation, but had not notified the president or the prime minister. Fidan's movements and those of some senior military officers just prior to the coup attempt were later noted to be unusual. Many of the soldiers reported that they had been told they were conducting a counter-terrorism exercise.

The poor coordination and support as well as many tactical errors, such as the failure to truly secure communications and principals, as well as other basic elements of a coup, were surprising for a sophisticated military. It was theorized that the many failures may have been the result of forced early execution due to Fidan's discovery, but the minimal damage and strange choice of targeting the parliament and other key structures as well as the many other weaknesses and oddities in execution were striking.

Some speculated that a group within the military had planned to take action in anticipation of appointments to be made at the biannual meeting of the Supreme Military Council in August that would likely remove some from power. Suspected Islamists were regularly expelled at this meeting; however, this had declined in recent years, as well as the public prestige and tolerance of the military as a state actor, which irritated some Kemalists in the military and could easily have led to some restiveness.

Theories abounded, also including the notion that it was a false flag effort of the government. In many ways, it could be argued that the coup seemed designed to fail and serve to frame the Gülen movement as well as weaken the view of the military, thereby granting numerous opportunities to the government, including renewed calls for the extradition of Gülen. There was more than one comparison to the infamous Reichstag fire. The main opposition leader called it a controlled coup. Later, evidence emerged that appears to support the idea held by some in Türkiye and abroad that Erdoğan at least knew what was going to happen and allowed it to proceed in order to have a pretext for one-man rule.

What is clear is that there was vehement popular rejection of an undemocratic means of a change of government, mostly from Erdoğan supporters, but also from some who did not like the president. This surge of support was invaluable to Erdoğan.

As expected, Erdoğan immediately announced that the perpetrators of this unusual coup attempt were members of the fictitious terrorist group "FETÖ" and even alluded to Western assistance. The attempted overthrow was indeed a gift to Erdoğan, though it caused great pain to the populace. Two enemies, the military and the Gülen movement, had been denounced and marginalized.

Gülen immediately and repeatedly denied any involvement, writing "I condemn, in the strongest terms, the attempted military coup in Turkey," in a statement reported by *The New York Times*. "Government should be won through a process of free and fair elections, not force. I pray to God for Turkey, Turkish citizens, and all those currently in Turkey that this situation is resolved peacefully and quickly. As someone who suffered under multiple military coups during the past five decades, it is especially insulting to be accused of having any link to such an attempt. I categorically deny such accusations." He also said, "My philosophy—inclusive and pluralist Islam, dedicated to service to human beings from every faith—is antithetical to armed rebellion."

Of course, Gülen's remarks were not even reported in Türkiye and few but his own followers even heard the denial. The alleged treachery of the Gülen movement became the excuse for all manner of authoritative actions.

A state of emergency was declared on July 20, 2016 and gave the government unlimited power to circumvent many civil rights and protections. Immediately, tens of thousands were purged and detained, including not merely military officials, but police officers, judges, governors, civil servants, teachers and academics, as well as individuals in the private sector and other civilians. The swiftness of the response more than suggested that lists of

CHOICES

political opponents had been prepared in advance. Furthermore, there were names of individuals who were deceased on various government decrees. There were numerous accounts of torture and private retribution or discrimination. It was open season. More began to flee the country.

Erdoğan now had the opportunity and license to consolidate power and pursue virtually anything he chose to. He began to systematically dismantle institutional opposition across the entire spectrum of the constitutional system, gaining more control over the judicial, police, and military structures, as well as other spheres of influence. This was largely accepted, though there was little ability to even blunt his efforts.

"FETÖ," the made-up terrorist organization, became public enemy number one. Even liberals adopted the narrative. The movement was now blamed for not just the coup attempt, but events dating back years, including the murders of Hrant Dink and Christians as well as other scandals and destabilizing events. Gülen and a nefarious web of supporters were alleged to be omnipresent and behind virtually everything. The formidable deep state had been redefined. To this day, accusations and arrests continue. Millions of lives have been devastated.

The government used the emergency powers assumed after the failed coup to order the *Zaman* newspapers closed by decree on July 27, 2016. Most of the staff had already been summarily fired and the papers had ceased to be independent months earlier, but now it was more valuable to simply kill off even another government mouthpiece and sell or convert the available assets. Ironically, the large office building in Istanbul was

219

eventually transformed into a judicial annex. Many other media outlets and other businesses were also shuttered on spurious claims or because they had become tainted.

Reactions from the West were muted and mixed. While no doubt some might have liked to have seen Erdoğan deposed and some had doubts about the coup attempt, he was also the "devil you know" and they expressed support only for the democratic process and the rule of law. Many Turks resented what they perceived as a lack of solidarity and understanding of the magnitude of the events. Even veiled criticism of Erdoğan's sweeping action in the aftermath was seen as offensive. Russia, Iran, and others unconcerned with democracy cheerfully supported Erdoğan.

Interestingly, Lt. Gen. Michael Flynn, who would go on to become U.S. President Donald Trump's national security advisor for a brief period, publicly lauded the coup attempt as it occurred, decrying the dangers of Islamism, and we now know that very soon afterwards he began working for the Turkish government. Contracting with a blatant Islamophobe may seem odd, particularly at that time, but he was willing to lobby for the extradition of Gülen and even perhaps abduct and rendition him. The extradition case was a priority for Erdoğan, but for years, the government has never been able to produce sufficient evidence. There was also a sense of irritation or lack of understanding that the U.S. president does not have the constitutional authority to simply order an extradition, but while frustrating for Erdoğan, it also provided him with a useful populist point of rhetoric.

Flynn was undoubtedly seen as a potentially useful ally in Washington with regard to Gülen; U.S. support for the Kurdish People's Protection Units in Syria, which Türkiye views as a wing of the PKK; the cases related to Reza Zarrab and Turkish banking officials; as well as other matters. A typically practical exception was made for a marriage of convenience. Though Erdoğan blasted Trump's Islamophobia, he recognized the unprincipled, transactional nature of his presidency and sought to take advantage of the opportunities it presented.

The alleged terrorist organization "FETÖ" has not been recognized by any state party to the European Convention on Human Rights (all Member States of the Council of Europe) or the U.S. Only Northern Cyprus (2016), Pakistan (2018), and the Gulf Cooperation Council and Organization of Islamic Cooperation (2016) have given it an official designation. In fact, the European Commission, the U.S., and others have repeatedly noted credible allegations of persecution, torture, and mistreatment in Türkiye and extending to transnational repression. In June 2023, PACE echoed the findings of U.N. groups and others and found that Türkiye relied upon various means, including violence, to silence dissenters living abroad.

For example, teachers and educators were abducted from Pakistan in October 2017, and the mainstream media in Türkiye sadly portrayed these innocent people as if they were dangerous criminals. Many others have been maligned, stalked, threatened, and attacked.

The period that followed the aborted coup was hellish. I was safer than I would have been had I been in Türkiye, but of course my family was still there, and I was watching a daily exercise in mob mentality. I was active on social media and condemned all coup attempts as well as the collective punishment and demonization of the movement. Pro-Erdoğan trolls, who had already been hateful to government critics, had now been emboldened and the insults and threats intensified. The general public had now been incited to open, explicit hatred.

Finally, I realized that it was pointless and even ill-advised to speak or write on these subjects in Turkish. People were not willing to listen to me, even as I acknowledged mistakes made by the movement or repeated that anyone breaking the law should be held accountable. The government narrative of a contrived "FETÖ" was firmly established in society. It had been remarkably easy to stoke the existing fear, distrust, and prejudice and distract from legitimate governance failures and other grievances. There was now a target for venting any and all frustration. Economy is poor? "It's a FETÖ plot!" Didn't get a job you wanted? "FETÖ is responsible!" And so on.

Even before the coup attempt, some of my friends had distanced themselves from me and others because of the stigma and threat posed by the association. After July 15, 2016, many unfriended me on Facebook, and thousands unfollowed me on Twitter. I could understand the fear, but it was interesting to see this from even some self-proclaimed liberals and critics of the regime. It became a sort of litmus test for me. I truly understood the reticence due to possible retribution, but I also learned who people really were and how much they believed in their principles. I also noted the recriminations and expressions of "It's your turn now," referring to Gülenist support for some equally unjustified prosecutions in the Ergenekon trials and other issues. But rational discussion was sadly impossible. I eventually stopped commenting even in English for some time because it was of no use.

After the failed putsch, it became even more difficult to follow events in Türkiye. The young reporters who had been working for *Turkish Minute* from Türkiye left the job due to a justifiable fear. There were even violent repercussions in Belgium and elsewhere abroad. Overnight, anyone with any real or imagined connection to the Gülen movement could be declared a terrorist and face dramatic consequences. Erdoğan was following through on his promise to demonize and destroy the movement.

It was expected that the regime would move against journalists, key businessmen, and civil servants, but no one thought the purge would extend so broadly to innocent employees and family members. The purge was much worse than anticipated. The coup attempt had provided Erdoğan with a perfect pretext. Illegal profiling in the bureaucracy was nothing new in Türkiye, but the scale of the reprisal against the movement was—and continues to be—immense.

The casual destruction of the lives of so many innocent people infuriated me. Teachers and others were detained and jailed by the thousands on terrorism charges, but society was largely silent. I was watching from afar, doing what I could to bring attention to injustice and simply encourage reasonable thinking, but I despaired not just for these victims but for what this meant in broader terms about my country and its future.

Zaman reporter Büşra Erdal was among those detained in late July 2016. I was surprised that she had stayed in the country once the newspaper had been appropriated. She had said a year earlier that members of Ergenekon were trying to reverse the judicial cases against them and imprison those who had pursued them. She had expected a vendetta from the deep state. When a court ordered that she be released from prison, some well-known journalists, İsmail Saymaz and others, lobbied for her re-arrest on social media. This pattern was seen many times. In Türkiye, social media users and government supporters can have greater influence than the courts.

Saying goodbye to my mother in Brussels, July 2016

July 27, 2016 was a big day for me. I was to leave Belgium to begin my fellowship in New York and I was excited. However, that morning, I woke up to a direct message from a neighbor in Istanbul. In the early hours, the police had arrived with an order for my detention and searched our family apartment. I learned that they had taken some of my books as "evidence." The title of one book included the word "darbe," which means "coup" in Turkish. I had always laughed when I heard old stories about dissidents arrested for innocuous items, such as a red light bulb, which supposedly indicated support for communism. Apparently, not much has changed. Our neighbor asked me to delete our messages as a safety precaution.

Fear and uncertainty were rampant. I felt terrible that my family had to go through that, but fortunately, no one was detained or arrested. This is common practice when the wanted targets are not found. As just one example, the wife of Bülent Korucu, long-time editor-in-chief of the political weekly *Aksiyon*, was taken into custody and jailed when the police did not find him at home at the time of the search.

I made my way to the airport in Brussels with this frustration and sadness weighing on my heart. I was worried that my passport might have already been canceled by the Turkish government. I felt a wave of relief as I went through passport control and let out another deep breath once I took my seat on the United Airlines flight to Newark, New Jersey. I texted a few friends to report that there had been no difficulties. But when a flight attendant approached me just minutes before departure, my heart sank. I knew what was about to happen. She asked me to gather my belongings and exit the plane. Of course, everyone stared as I collected my things and followed the flight attendant to the door. I felt like saying out loud, "I am a journalist and the regime in Türkiye has probably unjustly invalidated my passport."

Once I had deplaned, I went to the police station inside Zaventem Airport to see what I could do. The precise circumstances were a bit unclear. While in the waiting room, I called my former co-worker Celil Sağır, who had relocated to France, and I could not help but cry. I felt utterly hopeless.

The police took my passport because it appeared to have been canceled. The officers said that this was becoming common for Turkish citizens. When they realized that I had a residence permit for Brussels, they seemed relieved. They said I could go home to my apartment, but Brussels did not feel like home. I was supposed to be starting a new life in the U.S. Now I was stranded in Belgium for who knew how long with the worry of a request for extradition and facing imprisonment as a terrorist.

After I collected my meager luggage, which contained all that I had, my colleague from *Zaman*, Kavak, came to the airport and took me to his family home next door to my own apartment. Gültaşlı and his wife, Neslihan, also came to confer about what to do. They were always very supportive during my time in Belgium. After listening to the comforting words of my friends, I went back to my apartment, but I was in a state of something like mourning. It was very painful to be helpless and feel lost. For about a day, I did not unpack more than the minimum necessary. Instead, I grieved and listened to sad Turkish music.

Gültaşlı contacted friends at EU institutions for help or guidance. For the first time, I began to think about asylum. I realized that it would be extremely stressful to live with the uncertainty of a residence permit that was tied to a very fragile company. Friends at CPJ stressed that my safety must come first. The prominent British journalist Tim Sebastian often wrote to me to ask how I was doing. I will always appreciate his solidarity. More and more I internalized how little nationality means; it is humanity and universal values that matter. My fellow

CHOICES

Turks had labeled me a "terrorist," but I received sympathy and assistance from foreigners.

I was still completely depressed and feeling sorry for myself when a friend, political scientist Gökhan Bacık, who had also left Türkiye due to the increasing repression, introduced me to an acquaintance one day. I did not realize it at the time, but the thought was that we might be a potential match. This Turkish friend of his who had been in Belgium for years took us to a museum in the center of town, but I was so downcast that I did not pay any attention to this new man at all.

When dropping me off at home, he commented that everyone has problems and struggles in their life and mentioned his difficult divorce. I found the comparison of so many losing everything to more ordinary challenges a bit frustrating, but he was kind and I thought I had nothing to lose by getting to know him, especially at a time when I was feeling so bereft.

I had no expectations, but when he soon took me to dinner at a beautiful castle, I felt better for a few hours. He seemed like a decent guy and he treated me like a lady, which felt really good. After a few dates, and with the encouragement of my family and some friends, I thought it might be time to prioritize my personal life.

This man was respectful and affectionate, and though his family was Turkish, he lived in Europe and seemed Western in many ways by Turkish standards. Yet I could not imagine living in Belgium married to this man. It would offer me a home and stability, and I wanted to give the relationship a chance, but I also knew that I was reluctant to rely on anyone and did not want to make a poor decision when I was emotionally susceptible and needed security.

About 10 days after my passport was confiscated, I called the police to inquire about my status. They said that my passport seemed to be valid after all, and that I would be permitted to travel. I was relieved, but felt I had to make a decision about my future quickly because I knew that anything could change overnight.

I was nervous about the prospect of a lonely life far away in the U.S. with no clear plan, since it was now too late to take up my scholarship, so I decided to stay in Belgium for the time being. I had an opportunity to become a permanent resident if my relationship led to marriage, but I still did not feel comfortable with this. I reluctantly decided to apply for asylum, which would offer me some legal protection and time to assess my situation more clearly.

Above all, I needed safety. I still felt some hesitancy about pursuing an asylum claim as I struggled with my doubts and emotions, but as a Kurdish activist I met in Brussels said, "Sevgi, my friend, asylum is an honor," which helped me to change my view.

Much later, through a lawyer, I saw the official request sent by the Turkish government for my extradition from Belgium. I had officially been added to a list of wanted terrorists. Fortunately, Belgium refused deportation, citing my approved residence there.

CHOICES

Belgian denial of request for extradition to Türkiye, July 2016

The hours I spent in the asylum center in Brussels before eventually submitting my application in September were a very humbling experience. Standing in long lines for fingerprinting, a chest X-ray, vaccinations, and other scrutiny, I felt like it was happening to someone else. It was surreal. Waiting at each step of the process with refugees from Afghanistan, Iraq, Syria, and other war-torn and struggling parts of the world brought it home to me that anyone can become a refugee. I more fully understood some of what people forced to leave everything and live without a country feel.

229

Again, I thought to myself how swiftly and utterly my life had changed. Just a few years earlier, I had been traveling on the Turkish presidential plane with a diplomatic passport. Now, I had been classified as a terrorist and was about to relinquish my passport to flee persecution. I felt resentment and great sadness at the way my own society and government had treated me and so many others. I knew it would not be easy, but I preferred a mediocre life in the free world to a position of power in such contemptible circumstances.

In Türkiye, the effort to brand and blame the Gülen movement had taken on enormous proportions. All of the major TV channels, including international affiliates CNN Türk and Fox TV, parroted Erdoğan's narrative, despite their supposed standards. They could not have survived otherwise, but the media defamation campaign has been extremely effective and destructive. The slightest association with the Gülen movement, among other "crimes," was and remains sufficient to bring on pursuit and suffering.

Possession of Gülen's books was now considered evidence of participation in terrorism, and even more absurd excuses were now ordinary. I was especially disappointed by the response of intellectuals. A populist reaction was one thing, but I was profoundly frustrated by the lack of resistance from many who knew better but remained quiet. I wrote about this when *The New York Times* again asked me to contribute an opinion piece. Cem Küçük, one of the most hateful pro-regime columnists, joined the furious fray online and elsewhere, calling me a terrorist and other vile names and demanding my arrest.

Once I stopped posting on social media even without commentary or engagement, I felt less stress from that kind of vitriol, but I continued to have nightmares about Türkiye. The themes were always similar: being stuck there, fear of being informed on, being arrested, not being able to flee. I still have these nightmares, though less frequently now.

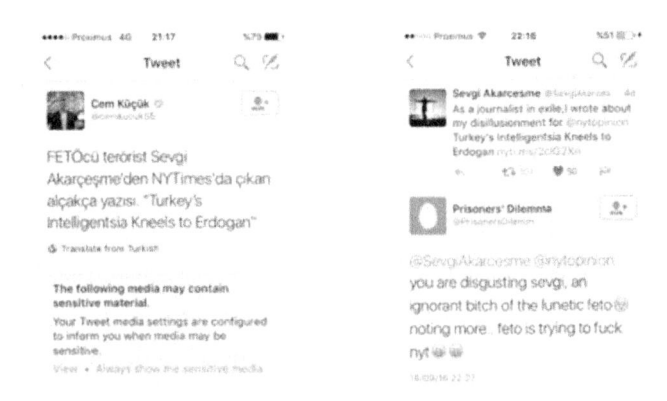

Some of the Twitter (X) posts directed at me, September 2016

The massive propaganda against the Gülen movement had convinced many that even teachers they knew personally who taught their own children were part of an elaborate, shadowy terrorist network. Given these circumstances, people began to leave the country en masse. Journalists were among the first to flee because they were targeted immediately and knew all too well what might happen. But it was more than those who were at greatest risk; a significant brain drain occurred because conditions were not promising for anyone.

SEVGİ AKARÇEŞME

In August, I met some colleagues from *Zaman* in a small Belgian village. They had all fled Türkiye and faced great hardship, but that was secondary. We all felt that even the worst exile was better than trying to remain at home. But thousands of others who stayed were also vilified and had their lives upturned, often with extreme effects. It did not matter if the suspect was gravely ill. Mothers and infants were taken into custody. There were no boundaries. Even a comedian, Atalay Demirci, was charged with attempting to overthrow the constitutional order and being a member of an armed terrorist organization for tangential links to the Gülen movement. He was imprisoned for a time and the trial went on for several years.

I had decided to stay in Belgium, but I still had second thoughts and secretly harbored disappointment about not going to the U.S. It was not only a long-held desire, it also made sense, if only because of my knowledge of English. I had begun to learn French to be more comfortable in Brussels, but I knew it would take me years to become fluent. I again questioned and regretted returning from the U.S. after graduation from Temple University, but I knew then that my employment prospects as a foreigner with a degree in political science were limited, and I had truly missed Istanbul and my family and hoped to contribute to what had seemed to be a promising future for my country. At that time, there had been no compelling reason for me to become an emigrant.

In the fall of 2016, friends in exile and a business backer supported the effort to sustain and improve the *Turkish Minute* website. I was leading the effort to produce content and writing stories full time along with my colleagues because we had only minimal resources. My little laptop was now my office.

The volume and content of news out of Türkiye was crazier and more miserable than ever, and we often had to write stories in English without editing. A former colleague at *Today's Zaman*, Fatma Dişli Zıbak, also contributed from Germany, but in the early days, she did not even have her own computer. She borrowed one from a friend, but the German keyboard slowed her down. We all realized just how valuable the resources we had enjoyed at *Today's Zaman* had been.

As the horror at home continued and I saw so many struggling, I experienced severe depression coupled with thoughts of how fortunate I had been to be able to leave. Every day, former co-workers, acquaintances, and others I didn't even know were detained on spurious charges. I would wake up each day and anxiously check my messages to see who had been arrested. It was extremely difficult to bear.

CHAPTER 22

I did not know anything about the details or who might have been involved in the July 15 coup attempt, but I did not believe the Turkish claims that it was a Gülenist plot. Many Western media reports concluded that the coup attempt was not orchestrated by Gülen, but that some people associated with the movement were apparently involved. Gülen quickly called for an international investigation and denounced any supporters who might have participated. To this day, we still do not know definitively who planned the coup, although there are growing indications suggesting that Erdoğan knew about it in advance and that Gülen may also have had some foreknowledge of events.

Former *Zaman* reporter Ahmet Dönmez began to investigate possible Gülenist involvement. Unfortunately, he was shunned by many within the movement, yet he was able to reveal much that had been unknown about events leading to that fateful night.

According to Dönmez, there was a group close to Gülen who manipulated and possibly defrauded him. A man named Mehmet Değerli had apparently been introduced to Gülen as a liaison to the armed forces months prior to the attempted coup. It seems that he and a small group of intimates may have convinced Gülen that the military was preparing a coup d'état under the leadership of Chief of General Staff Hulusi Akar and that Gülen may have given at least tacit support by not publicly opposing the idea.

Many devout supporters rule out the possibility of fooling Gülen, and there is some speculation that Değerli may have been a government intelligence agent, but it would appear that Gülen may have been willing to, at the very least, stand by and allow the purported effort to remove Erdoğan. This would be acting as a political figure, rather than a religious leader, and for me, the lack of a candid accounting to his supporters in the immediate aftermath and to this day was enough reason for me to disengage from the movement. It is my opinion that he had a moral obligation to examine and explain the circumstances that led to so much upheaval.

When I think back to my conversations with Gülen in the spring of 2016, a detail has a possible new significance. He had said in April that his hopes for a positive change in Türkiye had been dashed recently. I wanted to follow up at the time, but the subdued atmosphere given our recent ordeals and difficult situation discouraged me from asking questions. His comment may have been simply an acknowledgment of the government's brutal use of power and the collapse of any hope of influencing society in the near future, which is all I could imagine at the time, but now I wonder if perhaps he was also thinking about the coup attempt that would be carried out just a few months later.

As I read the timeline of events in Dönmez's remarkable series, I became more suspicious of some degree of prior knowledge of the 2016 coup attempt among the movement's top echelons. Despite all the many things that still remain unknown, it seems plausible that Chief of General Staff Hulusi Akar wanted Gülen to believe that a hierarchical coup attempt was being planned. Akar, a four-star general who had been brigade commander in several NATO engagements and supervised much of Türkiye's engagement in Syria, was among those seemingly taken hostage during the coup attempt and was subsequently made into a hero for his reported resistance. He then served as the minister of national defense until 2023. There was suspicion about the authenticity of his story of events almost immediately after the events of July 15, which continues to this day in at least some circles. It was noted that in his position he could potentially have unified disparate groups within the military if he intended to launch a coup, with or without the covert blessing of the government or others. The true nature of Akar's relationship to Erdoğan is a matter that merits additional examination.

I, like many others, regardless of affiliations, find a coup to be an unacceptable means of effecting change and it was disappointing beyond measure and simply unsatisfactory that Gülen and his inner circle chose to remain silent in response to Dönmez's investigative reporting. Gülen had previously called for an investigation, yet he offered no explanation of events to his supporters. While Gülen has repeatedly denied any involvement in the failed putsch and other activities, to me, that was not enough. The nation, especially those whose lives have been devastated, deserves a true and thorough accounting. Decisions made behind closed doors by a few—whoever they were—resulted in ruin for innocent movement sympathizers and others who were caught up in the events and the aftereffects.

I could have gone back to the Pennsylvania compound after the abortive putsch, but I think it would be pointless since too much remains unclear and there is little willingness to investigate from within, much less make any findings public. This is a pity. Though in truth, the movement has been so methodically demonized that any report limiting the movement's participation or even once again renouncing any who played a part surely would be repudiated by many, but at least then sympathizers could be given some clarity rather than suffer such trauma alone and in the dark.

Some experts have concluded that even if some supporters of the movement were responsible for or part of the coup attempt, it is absurd to think that tens of thousands of people were involved in a plot that, by its nature, is highly secretive. However, the unknown structure of the top level of the Gülen movement left its adherents extremely vulnerable to state abuse.

I hope that one day the full truth about the attempted coup will be revealed. As of now, there is considerable conflicting testimony and other evidence. However, what we do know with certainty is that millions suffered and continue to endure the consequences. I have been advocating for the victims for years now, but it is important to emphasize that I also demand that the movement leadership be held accountable. The regime in

Türkiye was already a mafia state, and Erdoğan acts as may be expected from a dictator. My bar for the movement was higher. To my profound sadness, I realized that the Gülen movement was not so different from other groups in Türkiye in terms of unwillingness to be held answerable.

While working for *Turkish Minute* in the months after the coup attempt, I answered many inquiries from international media outlets. One day, I was interviewed via Skype by a French journalist. She mentioned that she wanted to talk to certain people in the U.S. I asked with whom. She expressed concerns about online security and speaking openly, but when I insisted, she named Gülen. The idea that I could be a conduit to Gülen as the former managing editor of *Today's Zaman* was probably widespread, but it was entirely mistaken. I could only refer her to the Alliance for Shared Values in New York City, which handles all media issues on Gülen's behalf. Such is the lack of understanding of the movement.

Despite well-intentioned pressure from close friends and family and my own desire to find personal commitment and security, I decided that my relationship with the man I'd been seeing in Brussels would not work. I still could not imagine a long-term commitment, no matter how nice he might be. I was tired of struggling on my own, but I had vowed not to marry simply for the sake of a marriage, no matter how late it was or what benefits it might offer. By October 2016, I was back to my "factory settings" on my own again and trying to find my way.

Working virtually around the clock for a news website was tough, especially given the painful content of the stories, but I had no reason to complain when others were suffering even more. I was officially employed by a Belgium-based company, which was a blessing. As soon as I received my first paycheck, I moved out of the guest apartment that *Zaman* Belgium had provided. Fortunately, I was lucky enough to find a small but adequate studio next door. It was the size of a typical hotel room in the U.S., but it suited my needs, and I was grateful. As I adjusted to this new life, I became a little less depressed, but still often cried at night.

Physically, I was in Belgium, but I was surrounded by people from the movement and terrible news from Türkiye. My only Belgian friend was a lonely, elderly Flemish neighbor I helped when she broke her foot. I thought about the importance of personal connections and the role of community. This was an important cultural touchstone. I reflected on how those who are involved with the Gülen movement frequently get together as families, and as a single person I felt a little left out, but I knew that if I needed help, I would get it. And I did. With the accumulation of stress in the months that followed, I suffered from increasingly frequent migraine headaches. My Turkish neighbors once took me to the emergency room and waited there for me. I will always be grateful for their many kindnesses.

I will never forget the melancholy fall and winter mornings in Brussels. Even after eight a.m., it was still dark, and it took a lot of effort to get out of bed and start the day. I faithfully attended French classes and eventually earned my certificate, but I never really felt committed or truly engaged. I was thankful for all the opportunity and assistance I had been offered, but I realized that for me, Belgium was not going to be home. It was merely a safe refuge until I could find a way to the U.S.

I usually hurried home from language school to work for *Turkish Minute*. I worked in shifts with former co-workers located in various countries, such as Celil Sağır, Osman Ünalan, and Fatma Dişli Zıbak, but since I was also in charge of administration of this young venture, I had almost no free time. There was not a single day that I did not have a headache. Reports of the brutal purges and cruelties continued, and I had only depressing stories to report, including incidents of torture.

It was very hard on us all. I was glad that we had a safety net when it came to copyediting and more, thanks to the help of our chief copy editor at *Today's Zaman*, Helen Betts. The pro-government media assumed that we were a big team and had plentiful resources, but it was simply a huge effort from a small group with very little but determination and dedication. We were all overwhelmed, but hard work helped make *Turkish Minute* successful and something we could be proud of. It has continued to grow ever since.

On New Year's Eve, I decided to go to the Grand Palace with my neighbors for a change of pace and a break, thinking there would be a spectacle. I was surprised to find that not only was there nothing more than an aimless crowd, but most of the cafes were closed. While on the bus headed home, I received a text from Sağır requesting that I report on news of an armed attack on the posh Reina nightclub in Istanbul. Details were few in the immediate hours afterward, but apparently an ISIS terrorist had massacred innocents, including foreign nationals, who had been celebrating the start of the new year at the club. Many commented that the attack was yet another condemnation of the tolerance for and lax policies against jihadists in Türkiye in recent years.

On January 11, 2017, I turned 38. I did not really welcome it, mostly because I still felt adrift and lonely in a place I did not want to be. My Turkish friends were kind enough to organize a party for me, but I was depressed. While blowing out the candles, I made this silent wish: "Thank you, Belgium, but I hope I will not be here this time next year." Some of the first-generation children of Turkish immigrants I met in Belgium did not understand why I could not get used to or accept a life in Belgium. They had grown up in an entirely different world with a multilingual culture and had a fairly easy life in a welfare state. I had a different perspective; I was not there by choice.

One of the advantages of Brussels is the central location and easy access to any European destination. It was while visiting a friend in nearby Switzerland in late February that I learned that my asylum application had been accepted. I was the first among my friends from the newspaper to receive this status. I joked that being a single female journalist had finally been helpful. As soon as I could get a long-term residence permit in Belgium, I would apply for a travel document and rid myself of the danger associated with a Turkish passport.

I continued to explore various options for my future, but in March, my scholarship applications to Harvard and Stanford were denied. I had known that the odds were long, but I did not know of many alternatives at the time and so just tried everything. I was encouraged when Yale interviewed me for their World Fellows program and I made it to the semifinal round, but when I was still on the waitlist in April, my hopes for a quick resolution had been all but extinguished.

I decided to exchange my one-year Belgian residence permit and ID for a five-year version as a refugee. The Evere municipal official already knew me and had a warning for me: "Are you sure you want to give up your Turkish passport and become a refugee? Do you know what that means in practice?"

He was referring to, among other things, possible discrimination in Belgium, and he was probably right, but I was already aware that the chances of finding a permanent and satisfying job in Belgium were slim. I had also searched for a job in Brussels while seeking opportunities in the U.S. It did not take long to understand that I could not get a good job without at least knowing the local language(s). Even Gültaşlı, now a Belgian citizen and longtime journalist in Brussels, said that he could imagine having to become a cab driver or something similar.

The language barrier I faced in Belgium made me even more determined to take my chances in the U.S. I knew that, at worst, I could rely on Belgium's generous welfare programs, but I wanted to work and feel productive. I felt I still had something to give. I knew I would not feel satisfied or content without that. I was already feeling isolated and depressed. My only socialization was occasionally meeting people from EU institutions thanks to appointments made by my friends.

**Speaking at an event in Brussels, May 3, 2016
(I am seated second left)**

In the spring of 2017, I was invited to attend panel discussions hosted by the Belgian Parliament and the EP to talk about the situation in Türkiye. There, I vented my ongoing frustration with not only the government, but with the intellectuals of my home country. I will not forget the encouragement and support I received from EP member Rebecca Harms and Jenny Vanderlinden of Amnesty International in Belgium. Their concern for all victims, regardless of identity, was a great example and illustrated the fundamental difference between true humanitarians and many so-called human rights defenders who were selective in their support.

I was asked by some politicians about the future of the Gülen movement. I have never been in a position to speak on behalf of the movement, and I repeated my personal view that mistakes had been made in the past and perhaps more recently, but that there were a great many good people in the movement who were still suffering unjustly. They are my priority; I do not care whether the Gülen movement survives or not.

My understanding of the movement was that it had a mission to contribute to and promote a pacifist, modern version of Islam based on moral values through education, civil society, and personal service to the greater community. It was about raising good people, and I truly value the many sincere and generous people I met throughout my exposure to the movement. But importantly, I was very disappointed in the leadership of the organization and remain so.

Supporters deserve to know how decisions were made and by whom. I feel that their trust was betrayed. Unfortunately, as of the writing of this book, these questions have still not been definitively answered. Some supporters seem to be hoping for a miracle that will save all the victims of the purges, but that is unlikely, at least under the present regime, and to my mind, simply waiting is not enough.

Those with refugee status in Belgium were allowed to obtain a travel document valid for two years, and I applied as soon as I could. When I received the official blue document from the Kingdom of Belgium, I had mixed feelings. I had given up my Turkish passport, which had brought me only misfortune in recent years, yet I was not a Belgian citizen. I was merely enjoying the protection and generosity of a country where the rule of law prevailed. Now I was free to travel anywhere but to my home country. I dreamed of visiting places such as the pristine beaches of Greece, similar to those of my home, but I still had much to do to re-establish my life.

It was time to apply again for a U.S. visa. I was an active journalist, and my previous passports were full of U.S. visa stamps, but this time, I would be applying as a political refugee. In early May, I went to the U.S. embassy in Brussels for the second time in less than a year. I was employed and residing in Belgium legally, but I was still nervous when the consular officer asked questions. I could not claim asylum in the U.S., but I had no family ties in Belgium. In fact, I no longer had strong ties to any country. I did not know where my home was for a long time. It could have been anywhere I could find a steady job and preferably start a family, but at that point, everything had been demolished and had to be rebuilt.

After a short, tense wait, I was happy to learn that my journalist visa had been approved. I could not help but notice a difference in the attitudes of Belgian and American officials I had seen. Of course, they were just individuals, but the reluctance and negativity I encountered with a Walloon (a regional ethnic group) official contrasted greatly with the stereotypical optimism and friendliness I experienced with the American official. The U.S. embassy official even mentioned that I could use any valid visas I had secured earlier if I were to reclaim my Turkish passport.

Since flights within Europe were not expensive, I had already bought a ticket to Venice for mid-May, but once I had my visa, I could not wait to get to the U.S. Donald Trump had been elected president, to the dismay and consternation of many, and his contemptuous attitude toward immigrants was unmistakable. The "Muslim ban" had already alarmed everyone and nothing was predictable. I had thought that George W. Bush would be the worst U.S. president of my lifetime, but we were all soon to learn just how bad Trump would be. I always believed that the rule of law would prevail, but in the meantime, numerous people suffered from the change in immigration rules and attitudes. I was worried, but I was determined to try to make it.

Because of the bitter experience of being kicked off the plane the year before, this time I told only a few friends and family of my plans to go to the U.S. I was hoping to live permanently in the U.S., but I still wanted to maintain my ties to Belgium. It was the country that had taken me in during the most difficult time of my life, but I just did not see any prospects for myself there, and I thought that I would have more opportunity in an English-speaking country that I was already familiar with. I knew that Belgium would not be my home.

Thankfully, I was able to pay a fee and use the earlier United Airlines ticket I had purchased. On May 16, my Turkish neighbors and former colleagues from *Zaman* took me to the airport. We had become close during difficult times, and all my friends in Belgium had seen how unhappy I was. Despite the support of the Gülen community, I was often very isolated and felt out of place. In my very limited free time, my social activity was almost exclusively limited to a walk around the city, eating some Turkish food at one of the many kebab houses in the city, or going to the cinema in the Place de Brouckère. I had felt safe in Belgium, though there were many Erdoğan supporters and other potential problems there. Even now, when I think of Belgium, it brings back sad feelings.

I had left Türkiye with one large and one small piece of luggage. When I moved to the U.S., I still only brought two bags. I had been able to buy some basic items in Belgium, but life had forced me to live a much more minimalist lifestyle, and I had become comfortable with the idea of living with only the bare necessities. I knew what was truly important.

When I landed in the U.S., I was excited and happy, yet also a bit anxious. I had the proper documentation, and even my old passports as additional bona fides just in case, but I couldn't help but be nervous since this first trip with a Belgian travel document was so momentous. As the immigration officer joked and seemed unconcerned, I thought about differences between American and European culture once again. Despite Trump and others who have opposed immigrants throughout its history, American society has always been welcoming.

In the central square of Brussels, 2017

CHAPTER 23

May 2017 was the start of a new life. I was relieved and more comfortable in the familiar U.S. environment, but I still had to work hard to get my life in order. No one was offering me anything on a silver platter. I chose to go to New Jersey because I had close friends and a first cousin in the area.

A temporary stay at my cousin's house proved to be complicated and so I moved to the home of my old friend Nuray. She has a big house, but more importantly, she has a big heart. Over the years, hundreds of people have stayed in her spare rooms, almost as if it were a hostel. Both Nuray and her husband, Nasuhi, love hosting guests from all over and make everyone feel welcome. Nuray never even hinted at the expense, but since I might be a long-term guest, I decided to contribute to the bills and help her with things like picking up the kids from school and activities.

Soon after my arrival, I began to research my options for permanent residency. Some friends had received green cards through exceptional ability visas. The word "exceptional" intimidated me, but I realized that I might be eligible for this type of green card. I spoke with a number of legal experts and eventually worked with an attorney in Albany, New York. My case would turn into a long bureaucratic ordeal, but I was ultimately successful.

I also quickly realized how intense the last few years had been. I had already forgotten various events I had attended or commentaries I had written. The government in Türkiye had deleted the digital archive of our newspapers, but fortunately a senior administrative manager of *Zaman*, Mehmet Tahsin, had made an arrangement with the Stanford University Libraries to preserve the archive. I was given access to the collection and was able to retrieve what I needed. I do not know if Stanford has opened this record to the public, but I hope they will. Some news reports and other documents are still available online, but the full archive through direct links was expunged by the government.

The more difficult part of my immigration application was finding impressive letters of recommendation. No one from Türkiye could endorse my request for a green card because I was now considered a terrorist by my government. I did not even ask anyone from my home country, at least no one who was still in what had become something of an open-air prison. Fortunately, the connections I had made over the years through my travels around the world and my appearances in global media from Japan to Brazil were sufficient to supply what was needed. I realized once again how fortunate I was. Many did not have these resources.

Erdoğan also went to the U.S. in May 2017 and met with President Trump at the White House. Outside the residence of the Turkish ambassador, protesters had gathered in a peaceful demonstration to express criticism of government policy, particularly related to the Kurdish issue. When Erdoğan arrived after his meeting with Trump, some 20 members of his security team and entourage, who were used to casually beating protesters or anyone else—even grieving coal miners—at home, made the mistake of thinking they could do the same in the heart of Washington without notice or consequence. While cameras rolled, Erdoğan's staff launched themselves at the demonstrators and violently attacked them. Erdoğan claimed that the protesters provoked the violence.

The *New York Times* later published a chronology of events that confirmed what had been suggested at the time: Erdoğan had seen the protest and instructed his men to silence them. There was a notable reaction from members of congress and other officials. Numerous indictments were filed, and though Erdoğan's men were able to leave the country, they were subsequently unable to return to the U.S. for fear of arrest. This incident showed the world the audacity of the Erdoğan regime: If they can beat up protesters in the U.S. capital, can you imagine what they do inside Türkiye?

Indeed, particularly after July 15, 2016, torture had once again become commonplace in police stations and interrogation centers across Türkiye. The declaration of emergency allowed for an extended legal period of detention, restrictions on access to an attorney, and other measures that were easily abused. Reporters like Ayşenur Parıldak and a *Zaman* attorney, Ali Odabaşı, among others, were brave enough to speak publicly about harassment and torture during detention, but many stories remain untold or are limited to reports heard through friends or family members. The helplessness that I and so many others felt in the face of horrific stories was terrible.

When I visited the New York office of CPJ again that spring, Executive Director Joel Simon told me that I suffered from survivor's guilt. Many of the emotions I had struggled to deal with or just been forced to put aside came to the surface once I felt somewhat safe in the U.S. I was emotionally shattered and exhausted. I realized that I could not continue to work full time for *Turkish Minute*, especially because the time difference made it even more difficult. In order not to be a burden to the small, struggling company, I officially resigned without knowing what I would do next. I had to find a way to move forward.

In Belgium, I had not pursued professional forms of self-care, such as antidepressants or seeing a therapist. I thought at the time that a therapist in Belgium would not understand the extent of the insanity in Türkiye, and given the language barrier, how could I even begin to explain it? Instead, I had taken long walks through the Belgian streets and went to the nearest gym in Evere, thinking it would be enough. However, shortly after arriving in New Jersey, I began to feel extremely frustrated. So much so that sometimes I would privately even say out loud, "Life, I hate you! I despise you!" The dam burst.

I knew it was irrational and perhaps even selfish, but I needed to vent my anger at the unjustness of life. It was counter to the teachings of my faith to blame fate because that would mean indirectly blaming God, but I was overwhelmed at that point. I had returned to Türkiye from the U.S. hoping to have a normal life of a career and a family, but now I was forced to live in exile with nothing. I had no family with me, no job, no future prospects, nothing except my dignity. Many of my peers, on the other hand, seemed to be leading normal lives. Of course, outward appearances do not tell all, but it felt as though I was being unfairly punished. I did not really cry much, but I was very frustrated. I was also plagued by nightmares.

I finally realized that it would be beneficial to see a psychiatrist. I was very fortunate in that a female doctor who was close to the movement offered free services to victims of the purge. I offered to pay her some kind of fee, but she declined, saying that this was her way of helping. I will not mention her name because she wanted to remain anonymous, but I owe her a great debt of gratitude. She probably saved me from a lifetime of trauma.

She soon diagnosed me with major depression and post-traumatic stress disorder. I knew I was depressed, but I did not really think I had PTSD because I left Türkiye before the oppression peaked in the wake of the failed July 15, 2016 coup attempt. It took some time to acknowledge that I did not have to have been there to suffer and to recognize the toll of the increasing harassment that my colleagues and I had experienced for years. At the time of the final, brutal police raid on our newspapers, I had already felt that we were very isolated and that the destruction of the movement would be applauded, and the atmosphere only became worse after we were blamed for the coup attempt.

The doctor prescribed Prozac and after a few weeks, I began to feel better. I spent the holy month of Ramadan with Nuray, her family, and her many guests at fast-breaking dinners. I often wanted to isolate myself, but it helped to be around people. Even so, when I saw people laughing and living ordinary lives, I continued to wonder how they could laugh so easily and feel that life was actually a good thing for quite a while.

In April 2017, the referendum to approve AKP amendments to the constitution was successful, though with a very narrow margin. There were numerous irregularities, including an unprecedented decision by the Supreme Electoral Council to accept a large number of ballots that would ordinarily be considered invalid, but protests and confirmation of the illegality of this action failed. The office of prime minister was abolished and the parliamentary system was replaced with an executive presidency. The president was also given more control over appointments to the Supreme Board of Judges and Prosecutors. Everything was publicly justified as necessary for stability and success.

Advocacy groups reported that by the late summer of 2017, more than 650 known cases of children under six years of age were being held in jail with their mothers, and nearly a quarter of them were infants under the age of one. In addition, thousands of children aged 6-18 were also detained. Prison conditions were typically outrageous, and overcrowding became so egregious that other prisoners were released in order to squeeze in more of those remanded under the flimsiest of suggestions. Guilt by association or ridiculous "evidence" was sufficient to hold someone without charge. To my knowledge, none of the "modern" women's groups said a word about this brutal practice, likely because the majority of the victims were Gülenists.

Yet there was a general resistance to the ever-increasing authoritarianism. That summer, CHP leader Kılıçdaroğlu led a march from Ankara to Istanbul. Despite hot weather and literal obstacles in his path, Kılıçdaroğlu walked hundreds of miles to demand justice and the rule of law.

Thousands joined him to express their frustration with increasing injustices. The imprisonment of former journalist and CHP deputy Enis Berberoğlu on a scurrilous charge was the main motivation for the opposition march, but the crowds at Kılıçdaroğlu's rallies clearly suggested that there was a significant public thirst for justice.

Interviewing Kemal Kılıçdaroğlu, 2015

I awaited Kılıçdaroğlu's July 9, 2017 speech with surprising excitement. But as usual, he disappointed me, just like every other Turkish politician. Ironically, after calling for justice, Kılıçdaroğlu used Erdoğan's language and referred to the Gülen movement as "FETÖ." In other words, Kılıçdaroğlu was willing to call many thousands of innocent people terrorists, just as Erdoğan did. I was disgusted to hear this from nearly everyone, including Kurdish politicians who had protested being called terrorists themselves.

CHOICES

On the first anniversary of the failed coup, I visited Washington again to speak at an event organized by the Alliance for Shared Values at the National Press Club. There were still serious controversies and questions related to the events of July 15, 2016, including the role of the Gülen movement, but I was at least certain of the suffering of many innocent people and I wanted to speak on their behalf. I had been fortunate and escaped, and Prozac had helped to ease my constant grief, but I still had nightmares and felt bound to help others as I could.

The ceremonial recognition of the coup attempt in Türkiye was painful to watch. All year, it had been a constant theme, with rhetoric of a narrow escape and patriotic jingoism, exhibits of photos of those who died displayed in metro stations and on posters, the primary bridge in Istanbul was renamed for the martyrs of that night, and other efforts to relentlessly bolster more and more government control. Many Turks believed the rhetoric, but others recognized that the legitimate had metastasized into something else.

Things got so absurd that people wearing t-shirts that said "hero" were arrested on the preposterous grounds that it was a code or uniform used by the Gülen movement. Possession of a one-dollar bill supposedly indicated membership in the terrorist group and the serial numbers were alleged to have coded meanings. It was not uncommon for Turks to hold U.S. currency, and dollars were often gifted to couples at weddings or thrown over them in celebration, but it quickly became a risk. Others, including an elderly vendor in one case, were—and continue to be—detained and arrested for using the

ByLock messaging app, which was available on the internet for anyone to download, on similar accusations that it had been used by Gülenists. It became a rabid and fearsome witch hunt. No one was safe from potentially ruinous accusations.

However, it was essentially too late. There was nothing that could be done about it, and it was almost necessary for Turks to dissociate in order to survive. Even those who knew that this was farcical and worse rarely spoke up. Some have later acknowledged that many innocents were taken into custody.

Meanwhile, social media and tourism campaigns continued to make Türkiye look like a paradise. Visitors vacationed in Istanbul, the turquoise waters of the Aegean Sea, and other locations and shared photos of happy moments. It would be easy to believe that everything is fine if you don't read beyond promotional material. It was infuriating and debilitating. As I often say, Türkiye can be hell for its own citizens, but heaven for visitors.

I decided to take a few days off after the commemoration to change my mood. I went to California to visit a friend, Esra Kavurmacı. She and her husband had also left Türkiye due to security concerns. Her brother-in-law, a businessman and the son-in-law of the former mayor of Istanbul, Kadir Topbaş, had been imprisoned on charges of membership in the Gülen movement, released by the court for health reasons, and then re-arrested because of criticism of his release from a number of opposition politicians and members of the public on social media.

CHOICES

During that visit, I went on a date with a Turkish man who seemed interesting on paper. He was an intelligent academic who had also gone to Bilkent University, but it was yet another disappointment. I wondered, was I too quick to judge people, were my standards too high? Was I too demanding or difficult to satisfy? Was something else holding me back from finding love? I found no answers. It was a sore point that only increased my sense of desolation.

After my return to New Jersey, I focused on finishing my green card application. I was reasonably optimistic that I would be able to find a job in journalism or something similar once I had a work permit. I spent most of my time at home, searching for a job, writing for *Turkish Minute* again without pay, and following the deteriorating situation in Türkiye. I also began to work on this book as a form of therapy and went to fencing lessons with my friend's daughter, Leyla.

I was excited when my mother came to visit in the fall of 2017. Fortunately, she had been able to obtain a U.S. visa before the coup attempt, so there was no worry about new exposure or risk in that process. My brother accompanied her, as he is not independent enough to stay home without her. It was a bright spot in a bleak period for all of us. My mother liked the U.S. because of its dynamism, but she noted that Europe was more like Türkiye with its smaller stores and streets and more public transportation.

At about that time, I decided to try online dating. I knew that my specific criteria would probably make it difficult, but after all, I was already 38 years old and I was completely on my own with nothing to lose but my chains, to paraphrase Karl Marx. I signed up to a site under the pseudonym of Sara to avoid potential trouble with Turkish trolls, but after a few discouraging dates, I was soon convinced that the chances of finding a compatible life partner online were slim. What was I thinking? Nonetheless, I kept the account open, though I soon paid little attention to it.

In the meantime, I continued to have video therapy sessions with my Turkish psychiatrist. She listened to my endless complaints and resentments about the great injustices of life. I was fortunate that I found someone to whom I could express my deepest emotions and thoughts. I remember once saying that life really disgusted me. Even though I had tried to do the right thing all my life, I had ended up alone and in exile, with no prospects for the future. I was so angry at life that, no matter what I did, my anger did not subside. It was so hard seeing friends leading normal lives. Of course, I did not begrudge them happiness, but I wanted it for myself, too. I could not help but think that I was not expecting too much, just a reasonably ordinary life. Why couldn't I find it?

Even though I was not averse to the idea of living abroad, the involuntary nature of my separation from home was painful and complicated. I knew several people who had chosen to live abroad and build a life in a different country with greater opportunity. Others, like me, were forced to leave and deprived of everything we had achieved or hoped for. I also felt that some other victims of the purges were fortunate in that they at least had the comfort of their families when they made the transition, though that also brought different challenges. I was alone. Again. I had little beyond a small measure of professional and personal satisfaction. This kind of thinking may sound self-centered or unreasonable, but I think it is recognizable to anyone who has experienced depression, much less exile. I had absolutely no joy and little hope for the future, and it was devastating.

The continuation of daily horror stories from Türkiye only fueled my despair. Arbitrary arrests and dismissals were now shockingly familiar, but the forced disappearances, torture, and family separations were almost unbearable. All to preserve the fortune and position of a single man, his family, and selected friends. It was and continues to be very disheartening. It could have been so different.

I had sunk into deep sadness and disappointment when the opportunity for a two-week trip to five southern states helped lift my spirits. I joined a tour organized mainly by movement members that was intended to raise awareness about the situation in Türkiye. I had the chance to visit areas of the U.S. that I would likely at best have only passed through otherwise, such as Tennessee, South Carolina, and Georgia. We were delighted to find interest and sympathy, even in unexpected places. It was extremely exhausting to quickly go from one event to another following a rigorous agenda, but it was uplifting and I felt it was the least I could do for those who were incarcerated and all those still struggling at home. We were grateful for the opportunities provided and the media coverage in some locations that helped us reach an even larger audience.

My last stop on the tour was in Florida, the Sunshine State. When I had a brief opportunity to enjoy the warm water in Miami in early November, all the exhaustion washed away. It was my first visit to Miami, and I easily understood why people retire in Florida. I even thought to myself, "Since I have no home now, why not live in Florida?" Like many, I still think about possibilities for living somewhere warm in retirement, especially after experiencing the long winters of New Jersey.

That fall, in October 2017, another crisis erupted between the U.S. and Türkiye. The arrest of a Turkish-born employee at the U.S. consulate in Istanbul named Metin Topuz, who worked as a translator and assistant for the U.S. Drug Enforcement Agency, on charges of aiding a terrorist organization, espionage, and attempting to overthrow the government, apparently based on contact with police officers conducting the December 2013 corruption investigations, led to a months-long suspension of visa services between the two countries. Visas were soon reissued, but another U.S. consulate employee was also later arrested for alleged links to Gülen. The U.S. publicly supported the employees and stated that there was no credible evidence for the legal action. The already strained ties between Ankara and Washington were further troubled.

Erdoğan had good reason to become even more worried when it became apparent that Reza Zarrab, the Iranian businessman accused of being a primary figure in corruption and sanctions evasion, had made a plea deal with the authorities in the U.S. Zarrab's revelations threatened to be very damaging. It was horribly like a Turkish soap opera with a pop-star wife, corruption at the highest levels, and unending intrigue with significant political and economic implications.

Türkiye even issued diplomatic notes supporting Zarrab and did what it could to protect and support Halkbank Deputy Chief Executive Mehmet Hakan Attila. Erdoğan's fury was revealed when even the spouses and children of the police officers who arrested Zarrab were detained and Turkish media outlets controlled by the president spread the idea that the U.S. intended to use Zarrab against Türkiye. Zarrab's testimony was closely observed by some in Türkiye, but it had little real effect. The bank case linked to sanctions evasion is still making its way through the courts in the U.S., but it, too, will likely have little impact in Türkiye.

Trump's short-lived national security advisor, Michael Flynn, was also in the spotlight for his secretive work on behalf of the Turkish government without the required disclosure, including discussion of possible kidnapping. The extradition request for Gülen was repeatedly denied for lack of evidence, but it would remain a point of contention. I can very well understand how the Turkish government might come up with such a mafia-like plot, but I was floored to learn that a U.S. general and others became part of such madness.

As an indication of the preconception that prevailed, when an American TV program portrayed Gülen as a positive figure trying to escape the wrath of an oppressive leader, exiled journalist Can Dündar suggested that this was indicative of the movement's lobbying power. Once again, I was baffled by how a justly critical but biased journalist had become a poster boy for media freedom. The movement did have some representation in the U.S. and promoted its activities, but there was no basis for the aspersions leveled against it.

All the while, helpless sympathizers of the Gülen movement tried desperately to flee Türkiye. There were many tragic stories, such as that of a family of five, parents and three children, who drowned in the waters of the Aegean Sea during their attempt to flee. Apart from a few outcries on social media, there was deafening silence in Türkiye. After all, defending alleged terrorists could come at a high price. It was a stark contrast to the tears shed for Syrian refugees who also tragically drowned in the same waters, though that sympathy would ebb as well.

In early December, I was pleased to receive an offer to interview for a job with a nonprofit organization in Washington. Given my background, I knew that my chances for employment would perhaps be greatest in the nation's capital, but I also knew that there were too many qualified and overqualified applicants for too few positions. Then there was the fact that my career path had been unusual. The moment I was asked if I could travel to Türkiye as part of the job and I had to say no, I knew I had been eliminated from consideration.

CHAPTER 24

Something unanticipated and quite astonishing happened in early December 2017. One day before my membership to the dating site was to expire, I decided to take a look at my account to see what activity there had been since I had last looked at it. A nice-looking man named Mark had sent a message. His profile indicated that he had been born in Soviet Ukraine of Jewish heritage but had lived in the U.S. for many years and that he was divorced with children. I responded, but only indicated that I was about to cancel my account. He replied that he was impressed by my profile description, gave me his phone number, and asked me if I'd meet him for coffee. It was another bleak Sunday evening, and although I thought it would be another hopeless effort, I figured that I had nothing to lose and agreed to meet him at a nearby Italian pastry shop and restaurant the next day after he finished work.

I left home on Monday, December 4, 2017, to meet this guy named Mark with low expectations. When I arrived, I saw him waiting outside to help me park my car. It struck me as an unusual gesture, but one reflecting a desire to be courteous. My first impression was that he seemed to be a decent guy and our conversation was easier than I had anticipated. I remember feeling very excited as we got to know one another.

He had been a chemist in Ukraine and was now a successful professional in the pharmaceutical industry. He was smart and obviously hard-working, considering how far he had come after leaving Ukraine with nothing when it was still part of the Soviet Union. He was also considerate and seemed very interested and eager to talk. Just when he asked about a second cup of tea, I received a phone call. It was not a fake call to save me from an awkward date; unfortunately, I genuinely had to leave.

Although at the time I did not see this pleasant surprise as leading to a long-term romantic possibility, my internal voice urged me to put aside my hesitation and text him soon after we met. He immediately asked for a second date. I agreed. I liked him. Maybe I was ready for a change in my life. It still makes me uncomfortable to say this, but on that second date, I saw love in his eyes. He seemed like an extremely compassionate and truly decent man, and I trusted him almost immediately. In the days that followed, I quickly and quite unexpectedly fell in love with Mark. He regularly sent me sweet messages. After everything I had been through, I was content to enjoy it and not worry too much about our future for the time being.

I was already scheduled to go on a trip to Hawaii with Nuray and her family shortly after I met Mark. I was living off of my savings and worrying a lot, but I thought it was a special opportunity that I should not forego. I am still glad that I made that trip. The natural beauty of Kauai was astonishing. The breezes, perfect temperature, and abundant plant and animal life were truly amazing. The beaches, however, were not for someone who loves the calm waters of the Aegean.

Throughout the trip, I constantly exchanged text messages with Mark. Normally, I would have felt a bit sad to be on a vacation like that without a partner and be something of a third wheel, but thanks to his messages, I did not feel alone. I was happier than I had been in a long time. My awkward dates had previously been a fun topic of conversation with Nuray, but she had then said she did not want to hear about my dating unless it got serious, so I kept this exciting new relationship to myself for the most part. Perhaps she thought that matches made online were a waste of time or unlikely to be successful, but the attempts of my seemingly extensive network of friends to set me up had not been fruitful either.

Even though I was not thinking about a future together, I thought it was important to be open and honest with Mark about our differences. I told him that I am an observant Muslim and that I could not marry outside my faith. He is not particularly religious. For him, religion is part of an identity and culture, especially because he had grown up in a Jewish family in Soviet Ukraine, a minority that faced discrimination, but attitudes about Jewish identity in the former USSR can be quite different from those elsewhere. I believe he identifies as Russian more than anything else. To my surprise, shortly thereafter, he said that he had stopped drinking alcohol and had begun to eat only halal meat (broadly speaking, "halal" means permissible according to Islamic law. While not the same, it is somewhat analogous to the idea of the kosher laws of Judaism). Of course, I had not asked him to change anything. I was impressed that he had decided to make this commitment.

SEVGİ AKARÇEŞME

On Christmas Eve, Mark asked me about the requirements to become a Muslim. I explained that it was very simple: One must acknowledge that God (Allah) is the one true god and that Prophet Muhammad was his messenger. He then said he wanted to make this declaration of faith. When I asked him if he was serious, I could see that he was. He had already told me that he thought that Muhammad was the only prophet whose existence could be historically proven.

In a private ceremony of two, he said that he believed in God and His messenger, and that was it. A few minutes later, he asked me to marry him. How could I have said no to such a loving man who made such sacrifices for me? It also touched me that even though he already had children and I had not mentioned children at all, he said that he wanted to have a child with me. He was almost a dream come true, a man who told me everything I wanted to hear and quenched my thirst for real love. We were both over the moon.

Everything happened very quickly after we decided to get married. Since I would not live with him until we were officially married, we wanted to hurry and agreed on a date in February. My family, friends, and others were quite surprised by the news. My mother and my sisters thought that it sounded too good to be true. They were concerned about red flags I might have missed under the spell of love. And it's true; I was in love. I have always been very independent, but I loved the fact that he treated me with a great deal of care and protective tenderness. Even my older Turkish friends commented on how much he seemed to be in love with me. I loved being loved and expressing love in return. At last, I was happy.

CHOICES

Mark and I were officially married in a civil ceremony on February 7, 2018, a very snowy day in New Jersey, shortly after my 39th birthday. Though my family had been a bit skeptical at first, they soon came to approve of Mark after witnessing his love and devotion firsthand.

My father, as expected, remained somewhat cool about my decision to marry a foreigner, and he did not come to the wedding reception on February 10. I didn't really ask about it, but I know that he could have come, had he really wanted to. All of my siblings but one who did not have a visa were able to attend our small but joyous celebration.

I had always thought I'd want a summer wedding in Istanbul, but my perspective had changed dramatically. Having a small group of friends who had been by my side in difficult times felt far better than a big fat Turkish wedding with lots of relatives and others to whom I was not close.

I met most of Mark's Russian-speaking relatives for the first time at the party. My guests constituted the majority and they do not drink, but since it was unthinkable not to serve alcohol at a Russian/Ukrainian wedding, we compromised by offering drinks from a bar and this seemed to be a happy solution for all. My Turkish musician friends even played the traditional Jewish celebration song "Hava Nagila" as a courtesy to my husband's relatives. It was only during the festivities that I realized that we had not even thought about a wedding song. It was an informal affair, executed with little planning, no rehearsal, and lacked some of the usual trimmings, but it suited us just fine. It was a wonderful day.

Wedding reception, February 10, 2018

I began to feel like New Jersey was my new home and I was happy in my new life. However, shortly after the wedding, I had a series of health problems, one after another in rapid succession. First, I had a miscarriage. Fortunately, my mental health was strong enough at this stage to withstand this blow. Then, my doctor discovered a large ovarian cyst that needed to be surgically removed. Just as we were about to schedule the surgery, I fractured my right foot. I was stuck at home and not able to do much at all for weeks.

When I finally recovered sufficiently to have the abdominal surgery in August, I discovered that I was pregnant again. It was nerve-wracking for us, but fortunately our baby survived the procedure. When I woke up, the nurses commented on how obviously worried and dedicated Mark had been.

I had expanded my job search to include all kinds of communications positions, but it was not as easy to find a post as I had hoped. I began to work for *Turkish Minute* again while looking for a more stable, long-term career option. The purges and retribution in Türkiye had not slowed, and my home country continued to be a source of stress for me even after I had found happiness and established a second life. There has not been a single day that I did not worry about my loved ones and the many others in Türkiye who are suffering.

The state of emergency enacted after the coup attempt and used to crush opposition of all kinds in the name of national security and public safety was finally lifted in July 2018, and life was "normal," but very difficult. The emergency provisions had become something of a de facto norm in many ways. Executive decrees that provoked waves of dismissals, closures, confiscations, bans on assembly, and other violations of rights remained in place, and arbitrary detentions, arrests, and sentencings continued. Furthermore, the economy was struggling.

Erdoğan had managed to consolidate his power through convenient alliances and a weak opposition that did not and could not really pursue his many offenses. As of the writing of these lines in 2023, a lot has changed, yet virtually nothing has changed for the better in Türkiye since at least 2016. Erdoğan has survived several elections, countless tensions, economic crises, terrorist attacks, a coup attempt, and notably, a poor response to major earthquakes in February 2023, because he had established one-man rule.

I worked for *Turkish Minute* from home until shortly before my delivery. We welcomed our baby girl in the first hours of April 9, 2019. Mark had always wanted to name a daughter Sara, a classic name with multicultural appeal, and I added the middle name of Hayat, which means "life" in Turkish as well as Arabic. I had suggested the name

Vera, derived from words for truth and faith, but my husband laughed at the suggestion. Apparently, it has an unenviable rural connotation in Russian culture and might be considered old-fashioned in the U.S.

My life changed forever with this beautiful girl. I had thought that perhaps I was not meant to be a mother, and yet to my surprise, I loved almost every minute of it, even when I was about to go crazy trying to take care of an infant without a lot of family or friends around to help. The first six months were very demanding. I'm glad that I did not have to work during that time and was able to devote myself to creating a special bond and watching her grow.

With newborn Sara Hayat, New Jersey, April 2019

I soon resumed my job search but had no success. My husband suggested that I consider teaching. He spoke of the importance of education and the influence teachers have, noting that their role is often undervalued, but not entirely unlike journalism in that teachers contribute to a well-informed public. I agreed, and in the fall of 2019, I decided to begin by teaching English at a language school.

I took the language proficiency exams and the praxis required by the state for aspiring teachers. Fortunately, I passed both without difficulty. I received my teaching certificate in English as a second language in January 2020 and found a job the next month at North Star Academy, a charter school in Newark. I was excited and relieved to finally be going back to work again.

Unfortunately, at about that time, reports of something called COVID-19 began to appear in the media. A novel coronavirus that was highly infectious and caused a disease that was potentially deadly had begun to spread and cause alarm. It quickly became a pandemic and overwhelmed systems of all kinds around the world.

Daily life was disrupted as various measures were implemented by governments in an effort to contain the virus. The effects were enormous. Like most everyone else, I never expected to experience such a global crisis. In March, we began to teach remotely to avoid close contact. It was a challenging introduction to my new profession, but I am grateful that working from home allowed me to keep Sara Hayat with me all the time until she was 16 months old.

Despite my relatively low profile after leaving Türkiye, the regime did not forget about me. According to an official police document, the government launched an investigation of me in 2020 using familiar criteria of the purge, such as determining whether I or any member of my family had downloaded the ByLock app and if I had an account with a bank associated with the Gülen movement. Perhaps the bureaucratic machinery had not caught up to the fact that I was already out of the country and not likely to return.

SEVGİ AKARÇEŞME

ARAŞTIRMA TUTANAĞI

Zonguldak Cumhuriyet Başsavcılığının 22.09.2020 tarih ve 2020/5630 Soruşturma sayılı talimatına istinaden; talimatta belirtilen T.C. ▇▇▇▇▇▇▇▇ kimlik numaralı Sevgi AKARÇEŞME isimli şahsın ve ailesinin Bylock kullanıp kullanmadığı, şahıs hakkında Müdürlüğümüzde bilgi belge vb. delil bulunup bulunmadığı, şahsın Bank Asya isimli bankada hesap hareketinin bulunup bulunmadığı, örgütün üst düzey yöneticileri ile irtibatının olup olmadığı, şahsın örgüte müzahir otel, yurt vb. kaydının bulunup bulunmadığı, şahsın üzerine kayıtlı tüm cep telefonu hatlarının tespiti ve şahsın POLNET ve ÖSYM sistemlerinde beyan ettiği numaralarda Bylock kaydının bulunup bulunmadığının araştırılması istenilmiştir.

Konu ile ilgili olarak KOM Şube Müdürlüğümüz Bilgi Sistemi veri havuzunda yapılan sorgu neticesinde bu tarih itibarı ile;

1) Sevgi AKARÇEŞME isimli şahsın ve ailesinin Bylock kaydına sistemimizde rastlanılmamıştır. EK-1

2) Sevgi AKARÇEŞME isimli şahsın havuz sorgusunda; Sevgi AKARÇEŞME isimli şahsın İstanbul Cumhuriyet Başsavcılığının 2016/110288 sayılı FETÖ/PDY soruşturma dosyasından firar olduğu bilgisine ulaşılmış, Sevgi AKARÇEŞME isimli şahsın şüpheli sendika ve şüpheli şirket SGK kaydının bulunduğu bilgisine ulaşılmıştır. EK-2-3-4

3) Sevgi AKARÇEŞME isimli şahsın isimli şahsın Bank Asya isimli bankada hesap hareketinin bulunduğu bilgisine ulaşılmıştır. EK-5

4) Sevgi AKARÇEŞME isimli şahsın tepe yönetimi sorgulama sistemimizde Ankara Cumhuriyet Başsavcılığının 2014/37666 sayılı soruşturması kapsamında alınan 72 şahsa ait olduğu bildirilen 336 GSM numarasının 01.01.2006 – 01.01.2016 tarihleri arasındaki HTS kayıtları kullanılarak yapılan sorgulamada üst düzey tepe yönetimi ile irtibat kaydına sistemimizde rastlanılmamıştır.

5) Sevgi AKARÇEŞME isimli şahsın şüpheli otel (Asya Termal) kaydının bulunduğu bilgisine ulaşılmıştır. EK-6

6) Sevgi AKARÇEŞME isimli şahsın sistemimizde bulunan GSM numaraları yazımız ekinde gönderilmiştir. EK-7

7) Sevgi AKARÇEŞME isimli şahsın aşağıda ekran alıntısı alınan ÖSYM ve POLNET sistemindeki GSM numarasında Bylock kaydına rastlanılmamıştır.

The Turkish government's official request for an investigation, dated September 22, 2020

I have felt safe from physical threat in the U.S., but after speaking with another Turkish journalist in exile here about the Turkish government's attempts to harass and even abduct people like us and witnessing pro-government media following, photographing, doxing, and libeling others, in addition to requests for extradition and other measures, I contacted the FBI, just to be on the safe side. They took note of my concerns and told me that if a threat against me emerges, they would notify me and advised me to be vigilant. I knew well the experiences of others and have followed their advice.

In 2022, journalist Ahmet Dönmez, living in exile, was violently attacked while with his young daughter. Though the police could not determine the identity of the perpetrators, he is known for his investigative reporting on mafia groups and links to the Turkish government, and had reported death threats that included the phrase, "Don't feel safe just because you are in Sweden." There are numerous other examples.

I had been disengaged from the often incredibly toxic environment of social media for a while. The fabricated acronym of "FETÖ" had become ubiquitous and the entire Gülen movement had been thoroughly and even joyfully smeared. Indeed, use of the pejorative acronym became a sign of undemocratic beliefs in my eyes, but only a very few both inside and outside of Türkiye could resist either their own biases or the pressure of the regime to comply with the terrorist characterization. It was very revealing. And discouraging.

Retired political scientist and valued friend Dr. Ümit Cizre said to me that there are two tests that define a true democrat in Türkiye: one's approach to the Gülen movement and to the Kurdish problem. In other words, one must demonstrate an unequivocal stance of upholding democratic principles. Cizre had been a professor at Bilkent University when I was there, but I never had the chance to take one of her courses. She later taught at Princeton University, met and married an American, and settled in the U.S. We had long conversations during the pandemic and became close friends. Unlike so many other prominent political scientists in and from Türkiye, she has been vocal in her criticism of the current government. She now avoids visits home because of the not insubstantial risk of arbitrary accusations and punishment.

In the summer of 2020, I felt inspired to create some social commentary and share it on YouTube. I had opened a YouTube account years earlier when I was at Temple University to upload videos as a sort of personal archive, but I had not realized then that it would become such an influential tool all over the world. In places like Türkiye, Russia, and other countries living under authoritarian governments, it was even more popular due to censorship of conventional media. People in antidemocratic countries know that most TV broadcasts are all about propaganda and find alternate sources.

I began to broadcast content on YouTube primarily related to Turkish domestic affairs, international relations, and human rights issues. My channel still has only a relatively small audience of a little over 20,000 subscribers, and it may never be particularly influential, but the response has been positive, though I still encounter trolls occasionally. I hope that it is helpful and provides perspective. Yet despite my limited outreach, shortly after I began sharing content, the Turkish government banned access to my channel in Türkiye. To view the posts, Turks either need to use a virtual private network or change their country settings. There are many such prohibited channels in Türkiye; it is an effort to silence any critical voices. Similarly, news of potentially damaging events is often embargoed immediately.

CHOICES

After a while, I began to invite guests to speak on my broadcasts. Some of those I approached about appearing declined because of the associated risks, and others simply did not even respond. I can't blame people for being scared. The still-ongoing purges are not a joke. In the summer of 2022, a popular female singer named Gülşen was arrested on charges of "inciting hatred" for a joke she made about religious high schools. It was a joke in poor taste made to a friend, but there was a public uproar. I can understand how some may have found it offensive, but arrest was an extreme response. However, some saw this as an opportunity to punish the irksome "Turkish Madonna," a woman who had already gone "too far" by daring to publicly support LGBTQ and women's rights.

Imprisonment for alleged political activity has become something of a black hole in Türkiye. Political prisoners from all walks of life have been left to languish for years. Once you are arrested, you are left to your own devices and the whims of fate unless you are extremely well-known inside and outside of the country, and even then, there are no guarantees.

Despite international condemnation, Osman Kavala, a philanthropist and human rights activist, has been in prison since 2017 on absurd charges related to alleged efforts to overthrow the government first lodged with respect to the Gezi Park protests, then the July 15, 2016 coup attempt. The ECtHR and several other bodies have repeatedly noted the lack of evidence in many of these cases and the apparent intent to deter critics. Kavala has called it "judicial assassination." That's why I always tell people that their first priority must be remaining free. I never take freedom or other seemingly basic rights for granted anymore. In a way, my trauma taught me to truly cherish and appreciate the normal things that we all deserve. Like other authoritarians, Erdoğan was able to gradually weaken, control, or overpower all of the institutional and private bulwarks.

In the early 2020s, Türkiye was struggling with the effects of the COVID-19 pandemic, a deepening economic crisis, troubled foreign relations, and growing public dissatisfaction. Throughout 2021-2022, a former Erdoğan ally and mafia mob boss turned whistleblower living in exile named Sedat Peker posted several videos online that revealed what many had already surmised: Türkiye had become a mafia state in which President Erdoğan was the big mafia boss.

Peker's allegations ranged from rape and murder to corruption, drug trafficking, and the role of organized crime in political machinations and violence, and he implicated leading business figures, legislators, members of the media, and government officials, including the brother of Erdoğan's son-in-law, the former finance minister. The scandalous claims received a lot of attention and the ugly specter of possible ties between the state and organized crime rose once again. There were calls for investigation, but to my knowledge, prosecutors did little in the face of Erdoğan's control and vehement denial of the accusations.

Nonetheless, this atmosphere did not bode well for Erdoğan in the lead up to the presidential and parliamentary election to be held in May 2023, called one of the most significant elections in the world for the year in the international press. It was another test of the public's support for Erdoğan. The economy figured prominently in the campaigns, as inflation and the cost of living had become unbearable and left even those who had been comfortable struggling.

In addition, devastating earthquakes in southeastern Türkiye and Syria in February had killed at least 50,000 (many suspect the true count to be much higher) and the government had been widely criticized for both corruption in construction in an area known to be earthquake-prone and an inadequate response to the disaster.

Resentments surrounding the millions of Syrian refugees living in Türkiye also figured highly. Furthermore, the election was momentous because October 2023 would mark the centenary of the republic. Erdoğan very much wanted to be leader during the celebrations and firmly take the mantle of national hero from the country's founder, Mustafa Kemal Atatürk, who had established the CHP.

Though there was dissatisfaction with the selection of Kılıçdaroğlu, leader of the CHP, as the candidate to represent a fractious but motivated new group of six opposition parties that included former AKP Islamists and was supported by the Kurdish political movement, as the election neared there was some hope that just maybe Erdoğan and the coalition of the AKP and the MHP could be defeated.

The popular Istanbul mayor, Ekrem İmamoğlu, a next-generation CHP hopeful, had been somewhat sidelined as a rival to Erdoğan (and Kılıçdaroğlu) with arrest and trial for "insulting electoral officials."

Erdoğan had tremendous advantages in the contest, such as control of the media and other levers of power, including the Supreme Election Council. He railed against terrorist elements, meddling enemies from the West, and once again promised that his strength would prevail in standard paternalistic, populist messaging and identity politics.

The opposition warned of increasing authoritarianism and pledged to eliminate the executive presidential system narrowly approved in the 2017 referendum, to restore the independence of the judiciary and the central bank, and to reverse crackdowns on free speech and dissent. However, despite the use of social media and appearances by coalition surrogates, the opposition strategy was poor and their reach was limited.

In a nail-biter, the AKP did not achieve the required simple majority in the first round of voting, forcing the first run-off in the country's history in only the third election with direct voting for the president. Importantly, the vote share of the third candidate, ultranationalist and former member of the MHP, Sinan Oğan, had exceeded expectations, and he became something of a kingmaker. He ultimately supported Erdoğan, who was re-elected president in the second round with some 52 percent of the vote.

There was much analysis of the failure and plenty of recriminations among the disappointed opposition. The coalition had been an ambitious effort, but one built on fragile foundations and fraught with errors. It remains to be seen how the CHP and other parties will reinvent themselves in the future. For the time being however, Erdoğan's one-man rule is, unfortunately, quite secure.

CHOICES

I'm truly convinced that you can buy almost anyone and anything in Türkiye. The society has always been more corrupt and divided than I wanted to see or believe and has not managed to evolve sufficiently. I had confidence that it could transform and elevate itself to a truly Westernized society that respected the rights of all, but the populace has made a different choice.

I think their views have been manipulated, but also that they did not want to pay a price for equal citizenship, rule of law, merit-based promotion, and the like. Too many want shortcuts and do not object to—in fact prefer, in many cases—a strongman in power. Those who, while unhappy, accept the familiar, and those who aspire to be like mafiosos outnumber those who want to have the rule of law.

Much of the public is insufficiently aware of their options and the benefits of more democratic governance, and to be fair, they have not had much chance, but as a result, Erdoğan continues to rule and Türkiye slides further away from its potential. This is apparently acceptable to at least half of the nation. The other half is fragmented and unable to agree that basic human rights should apply to everyone.

Polarization would appear to be endemic. Divisions now largely overrule tolerance and empathy. Most everyone hates some other section of society and Erdoğan-type politicians foment and abuse the mistrust and bias to suit themselves, rather than encouraging a more mature attitude of peaceful coexistence. Thus far, other voices have been unable to overcome these barriers.

I have re-examined my thoughts about Gülen and the movement many times since I fled my home. It is another source of disappointment and resignation. I have realized that I trusted and gave too much benefit of the doubt to the movement based on the incredibly nice and generous supporters I have known and my own hopes for the positive change I thought it represented. However, the opaque leadership structure and the lack of transparency ostensibly designed to protect sympathizers was also an enormous vulnerability. It contributed to external suspicion and supporters were ultimately defenseless because we did not know who was making decisions or the basis for them.

In retrospect, it was poor judgment on my part to assume and have faith that Gülen and members of his inner circle, who are still unknown, would make good decisions. The mission, standards, and personnel in any organization may change over time, particularly when the influence of money and power comes to bear. It is important to be vigilant.

Though Gülen has admitted some errors while steadfastly denying any wrongdoing, it was a bitter disillusionment to discover that the movement has refused to accept even constructive criticism or engage in a candid self-assessment. Not everyone believes the government version of events, but I was wrong to believe that the movement was superior to any other ideological tribe. I am still convinced that the overwhelming majority of the people within the movement are honorable and well-intentioned, but the top decision-makers seem more and more dubious since they refuse accountability.

Public remarks made by an imam named Osman Şimşek also support my convictions about some degree of corruption in the leadership of the movement. He served as a kind of personal aide to Gülen for more than two decades until he criticized some controversial people around Gülen. In a YouTube interview of July 2023, Şimşek cautiously warned the movement about a clique of followers who were motivated by money and power and that they had misled and used Gülen, echoing the findings of journalist Ahmet Dönmez.

I have not considered myself associated with the movement since Dönmez publicized his series of reports on the circumstances surrounding the coup attempt of 2016. Many will confirm or support his conclusions in private conversations but refrain from speaking about it publicly to avoid trouble.

My social circle in New Jersey still includes some friends from the movement; some agree with my criticism, some refuse to talk about it. It is uneasy at times, but I don't want to sacrifice my few remaining ties to my past due to politics. More importantly, I know that they are decent people. We just have our differences when it comes to our perception of the leadership of the Gülen movement. Unfortunately, it would appear that the movement was hijacked by a few who still control some money and power. As long as they are not held accountable, the entire case is hopeless in my eyes and I will not participate. I only care about the victims who still suffer in Türkiye.

I have asked myself many times how I did not foresee the abuse of power and trust that occurred in the AKP government and in the Gülen movement. I accept responsibility for my defense of the early AKP and of the movement, but I would ask readers to consider the conditions. It was based on a hopeful idealism and a sense of purpose. I had a sincere belief that both offered the means to address long-standing deficiencies and to provide a positive progressive push forward toward greater democracy and development.

Atatürk redesigned the entire political, economic, and cultural configuration of Türkiye based on Western models. The rigid secularism of Kemalism rejected the Islamic faith that was part of life for most residents of the new republic. Only one identity was sanctioned. The assertive French-type secularism of the Turkish state created a fundamental contradiction that prevented the consolidation of true democracy. Much of the originally intended template for the future was abandoned or essentially a façade in practice.

The strains of rapid modernization, including both internal and external factors, also contributed to inconsistent development. Among them, linear progression was delayed by insufficient institutionalization and the dominating role of the armed forces in the civil-military relationship. A new class of secular Turks emerged triumphant while devout Muslims and others were denigrated and relegated to poverty in a kind of caste system. Religion then began to slowly resurface, and even the army encouraged a role for religion as a counter to communism, but it was to be strictly consigned to the margins.

Political decay and periods of instability further contributed to the rise of the AKP, the first political party with Islamist roots to achieve power, and a contrasting form of illiberalism. The unwillingness of the EU to accept Türkiye as a full member and the Arab uprisings of the 2010s encouraged a view among Turks that Türkiye could become a world leader on its own. However, the early economic success and promise stagnated and Erdoğan increasingly adopted an authoritarian style of governance. Broad acceptance of a strongman and weak allegiance to the core civil liberties associated with liberal democracy enabled a swing to a more conservative and intolerant attitude based on majority rule rather than shared institutional control, separation of powers, checks and balances, and the rule of law with protections for individual rights.

Democracy was primarily an instrument for Erdoğan. After all, he famously said during his tenure as mayor that democracy was not a goal, but rather a tool or a vehicle, suggesting that it could be taken up and used or discarded as needed. (The Turkish phrase, "Demokrasi bizim için amaç değil, araçtır," is poetic and catchy, despite its implications.) He skillfully used all actors and aspects of society to come to power, including exploiting religion. I am not convinced that his displays of piety are genuine. At the very least I would say that his attitude is pharisaic, as his actions betray the tenets of the Muslim faith on a regular basis.

Once at the top and unchallenged, his true intentions and priorities were fully revealed. It was not a state based on sharia law, but a pragmatic and self-interested one-man rule. He quickly moved to consolidate and retain power and accumulate wealth. Institutions were hollowed out, loyalty was given greater priority than competence, and corrupt crony capitalism flourished.

A cost of this hegemony, however, was a reduction in the capability to govern effectively and the country became isolated and beleaguered. The early benefits to the public evaporated. Failures in the economy and governance became visible and undeniable.

Erdoğan's solution was to redefine reality. He regularly claims that the nation's problems are not a result of AKP failures, but of its victories. He says that foreign powers and other plotters are envious and fearful. They conspire to damage Türkiye precisely because the government has done such a good job and the AKP is the only hope for the country to survive this racist assault.

Rather than address actual problems, he relies on addressing criticism of the problems. Outright lies, political astroturfing, and armies of government trolls are used to foment and cement social divisions and influence public opinion. These efforts are bolstered by brutality. The AKP does not seek to resolve issues, merely to overpower any opposition to its own enrichment. It follows a typical authoritarian playbook.

Türkiye was recently once again excluded from the most recent international Summit for Democracy. The annual EP report on Türkiye yet again contained criticism of a grim human rights record, including the arbitrary use of terrorism charges to silence dissidents, political control of the judiciary, mass incarceration, torture in police custody and in prisons, restrictions of free speech, refusal to comply with ECtHR judgments, abduction of Turkish citizens from outside the country, media and online censorship, a lack of access to a fair trial and suppression of journalists, social media users, opposition politicians, academics, lawyers, trade unionists, and human rights advocates.

Türkiye also ranked 117th among 142 countries and jurisdictions in the rule of law index published by the World Justice Project in 2023, and last among 15 countries in the Eastern Europe and Central Asia region. Each country's score is an average of eight factors: constraints on government powers, absence of corruption, open government, fundamental rights, order and security, regulatory enforcement, civil justice, and criminal justice.

Allegations of corruption in the Turkish judiciary have recently exploded. While accusations have been made previously, in October 2023 the Istanbul chief public prosecutor sent a letter with detailed allegations of bribery, nepotism, and other irregularities within the judicial system and named the president of the Istanbul Judicial Commission. This was followed by a decision from the Supreme Court of Appeals denying a Constitutional Court order to release an imprisoned opposition deputy. The law states that the rulings of the Constitutional Court are binding on all other courts and state bodies, yet in recent years, lower courts have failed to comply with the top court's judgments, particularly in cases with potential political implications.

The Turkish judiciary has been criticized by various international bodies for a lack of independence and for disregarding rulings of the ECtHR, which has jurisdiction to decide complaints submitted related to nations that are signatories to the European Convention on Human Rights. PACE, the parliamentary arm of the Council of Europe, has called for targeted sanctions on Turkish officials responsible for the unlawful imprisonment of political prisoners and other punitive measures.

Though there is appetite for change, the prospects for sufficient comprehensive improvement are unlikely in the near future. The always-heavy hand of the state remains both brutal and inept, and the institutional and cultural factors necessary to support a true democracy with tolerance of all expression appear to be insufficient at present. There are many genuine concerns and grievances, but the complexity and lack of will to truly address and reconcile a long history of pain suggest that drama and schadenfreude will continue for the near future. The victims change, but the desire for soundbite solutions persists.

As a devout Muslim, I had felt ostracized by secularists, yet felt no affinity for political Islamists. The Gülen movement provided acceptance and hope that we could find a way to move forward. Perhaps it would not be unfair to say that just as I have accused others of blindness, I too am guilty; however, I can say that I did not hesitate to openly acknowledge and correct my errors once known. I am faithful to my principles, not to personalities. We all resist recognizing cognitive bias, but we benefit from self-examination as individuals and as a society.

I now contend that Fethullah Gülen is neither a shadowy cult leader and terrorist nor entirely innocent. The AKP and Gülen had an alliance that served them both, but I believe it was never as tight as many think. There were various points of disagreement from the very beginning. Maybe Gülen had hoped to influence the AKP, but in essence, for both sides the relationship was simply useful, until it wasn't.

Little in life is strictly black or white, and we may never know the full truth about much of recent Turkish history. In any case, no matter what irrefutable evidence might be produced, some will not accept it. Fantastical conspiracy theories are sometimes more appealing and easier to live with than complicated and unpleasant truth. The deep state, at least now, may in fact be small groups whose membership may reflect changing alliances and opportunities to serve their own priorities by acting outside the law. However, the actual Turkish state would appear to be more and more involved. There has always been resistance to genuine democracy. Moral and ethical corruption is the real conspiracy.

Türkiye never succeeded in becoming a liberal Western democracy and the idea of serving as a model of a Muslim democracy was a tragic failure. There is still a reluctance to accept that an opponent need not be considered an enemy to be destroyed but as an adversary whose existence is legitimate and must be tolerated and even appreciated. Rather than fulfill its potential as an example of an early melting pot, the pot is melting. Achieving cohesion while accommodating various identities and appreciating the richness and opportunity they bring is a perplexing and frustrating struggle around the world. I fear that it will be a long time yet before fears, prejudices, and some justified mistrust are overcome and all voices are respected in Türkiye.

Though I love the city and country of my birth, I do not miss it. I only hope for the well-being of my extended family and all of those who live in such difficult circumstances. I hope that the pendulum will rest in a midpoint of equilibrium one day, but I fear that it will be long in coming. Change is occurring, but excruciatingly slowly and at present the weak cries for reform are largely smothered. Nonetheless, there are many of us who will continue to speak out and do what we can to encourage liberty and justice for all. The power of kings can be restrained by the will of the people—if they want to.

I now consider the U.S. my home of choice, though it too, of course, has its flaws and struggles with achieving democratic ideals. To be brutally honest, as we approach 2024 elections in the U.S., I'm concerned about the decay of democracy as never before. In that sense, I'm disappointed with a large segment of society here, too.

I hope to obtain full U.S. citizenship by the time this book is published, but the process has been long, arduous, and expensive. Navigating the inefficiencies of bureaucracy and finding reliable guidance can be quite infuriating. Nonetheless, I will persevere. It still represents a guarantee of rights that is not to be unappreciated. I look forward to traveling internationally again with that security. I have a lingering dream of spending the summers on the Aegean, preferably with members of my extended family. It may not be the beautiful Turkish shores, but if I cannot go home, I will continue to enjoy the beaches in other parts of the world at every opportunity.

I am grateful that my daughter will grow up in the U.S. in an environment that offers her more safety and freedom. She knows that Türkiye is part of her heritage and is learning the language (albeit somewhat reluctantly at present), but since we can't visit, for now at least, it remains remote, a story of both beauty and hardship, not unlike some of the fairy tales she enjoys. She is a clever, happy child and was born with advantages many do not have. I will do my best to ensure that she will not take these gifts for granted.

This book is part of my own catharsis, but also written for her. Understanding our history, in both personal and larger contexts, is invaluable. I also hope that others may find my observations useful and that we may avoid repeating some mistakes.

I no longer introduce myself as an exiled journalist, but as an ESL teacher. It appears that education will be my profession for the foreseeable future. I value the opportunity to contribute to the future of my new home and reinforce appreciation of democratic values. I will also humbly continue to do what I can to be a voice for those who are not able to enjoy their rights and encourage conversation and understanding in our effort to live together on this tiny, fragile planet.

A retired professor I know from Temple University, Dr. Conrad Weiler, whom I consider a family friend, has suggested that my background could be very useful if I were to become involved in U.S. politics, but I do not see that happening at present. But then again, you never know. After all, I could not have imagined my current life a decade ago. We absolutely have no idea what life will bring, but I will always know the value of freedom and the rule of law.

Despite all of the adversities, disappointments, and aborted dreams, I don't regret my decisions. I always did what I believed was best based on what I knew and I tried to maintain my integrity. I am content. I concentrate on the lessons I have learned and work on acceptance of what life offers and moving forward. I can now say "C'est la vie."

I have become more resilient and more wise. Though my faith in humans was severely tested, my religious faith remains strong and guides me. We have free will but are cautioned about personal responsibility and the pluralistic nature of our existence. As Jean Paul Sartre reminded us, the act of not making a choice is also a choice for which we must accept responsibility. While autonomy may be restricted by a government, an individual, or other factors, we have more choices than we may think. Every single day. It is challenging, but we learn and we grow with each step. Life is a test designed for each of us.

With Sara Hayat, 2023

ACKNOWLEDGEMENTS

I would like to thank all of those who helped me on my journey. I cannot mention you all by name, but I am truly indebted.

I also recognize that even those who taught me painful lessons made a valuable contribution to my life.

Additionally, I am very grateful to my literary midwife, Suzan Atwood, for her assistance in bringing this labor to life.